SCHIMMELPFENN

Roland Schimmelpfennig

PLAYS ONE

Translated by David Tushingham

OBERON BOOKS
LONDON

WWW.OBERONBOOKS.COM

First published in 2014 by Oberon Books Ltd
521 Caledonian Road, London N7 9RH
Tel: +44 (0) 20 7607 3637 / Fax: +44 (0) 20 7607 3629
e-mail: info@oberonbooks.com
www.oberonbooks.com

Cover image by Bill Knight of *Idomeneus* at the Gate Theatre, 2014.
Cast as pictured: Alex Austin, Jon Foster, Mark Monero, Susie Trayling and Ony Uhiara

Visit www.oberonbooks.com to read more about all our books and to buy them. You will also find features, author interviews and news of any author events, and you can sign up for e-newsletters so that you're always first to hear about our new releases.

Contents

'THE THEATRE NEEDS CHALLENGES'

An interview with Roland Schimmelpfennig

How did you get into theatre?

The initial spark – what I remember – was a show for children, *Around The World in 80 Days*, at the Deutsches Theater in Göttingen, my home town. I was six or possibly seven. Along with writing, theatre was always what I wanted to do. My friends and I made theatre together as teenagers. We had our own company. I really got started when I studied directing in Munich, but I gave up the course after two years when I was offered a full-time job as an assistant director at a theatre, the Münchner Kammerspiele. It was a lot of work, round the clock, eight days a week.

At what point did you decide you were going to be a playwright?

Writing – and writing plays – was always my objective. Training as a director, the years as an assistant and a dramaturg were ultimately a necessary diversion. By my mid-twenties I was ready. I couldn't stand *not* writing any longer. My desire became a necessity. I threw in my job at the theatre overnight and for several years all I did was write plays.

Were there other dramatists who you regarded as models?

Model is maybe too extreme. I tend to regard myself as an autodidact. But of course there are the great writers who open your eyes, who can invent an entire new world in just a few lines, who take your breath away – the writers I always go back to who I read over and over again and will keep reading. Shakespeare, how could I not. Lessing and above all Kleist were important. Far more than Goethe or Schiller. Georg Büchner. Peter Weiss. Beckett.

What did you learn from working with Jürgen Gosch*?

Stubbornness. Radicality. Freedom.

What do you look for in a director for one of your plays?

Stubbornness. Radicality. Being faithful to the text.
Precision. And freedom.

In The Animal Kingdom *the theatre is presented as a globalized, profit-driven business where individual artists have very little space for their own creativity. Does that reflect your own experience?*

Writing means freedom. As I writer I have never made compromises. On the contrary. The theatre needs challenges. Excessive demands. But that doesn't mean that the theatre is somewhere where you can go on ego-trips. Theatre is a collective process. It thrives on dialogue. Sometimes it's paradise and sometimes it's hell.

The idea that actors are 'free' is a big misunderstanding. Actors play a role. The only thing that matters is that there is a something of substance in their work, something like 'truth' – even if no one can say what that actually is – or whether it's purely about entertainment. Entertainment is often a shell without any content. Commercial theatre exists, of course. But that's never interested me. The theatre I love asks a few questions of itself and of its audience.

In the German-speaking theatre it's very fashionable at the moment to stage 'texts' rather than 'plays', where plot and characters are no longer so important. But in your plays you still tell stories. What is the attraction in that for you?

4

Stories are always about change. Or the desire for change. Or the fear of change. About yearning. About fear. About success and failure. For me the focal point of the theatre is always people, and people are what make theatre interesting for me, not 'text'.

Who are the people we see on stage in Idomeneus? *And why are they telling this story?*
Idomeneus is a collective story – told by many individuals. It is a kind of chorus, only here the chorus is fragmented, many-headed, contradicting itself. This chorus cannot be placed in a set historical or social category. The chorus no longer exists as a unit – perhaps because there no longer is any unified story or history. The chorus gets bogged down in variations, but none of the variations offers a way out. And that is precisely the reason why the chorus is telling this story. The past, the war, the human sacrifices overshadow everything.

Each of the plays in this volume contains repetitions or – more accurately – revisits certain moments in the plot again and again. I know no other playwright who makes such a regular feature of this and it's become a bit of a personal trademark of yours. How did you discover this technique and what are its advantages?

The repetition of the slap in *Peggy Pickit* is perhaps the most extreme example.

It's often important to me to examine certain aspects of a story over and over again together with the reader or the audience from different perspectives. Usually these are moments which are particularly painful, where you have put your finger on a wound.

Peggy Pickit was written in response to a commission for Volcano Theater in Toronto and you have recently premiered new plays at theatres in Tokyo and Copenhagen. Your plays are performed internationally and their subject matter is often international too. Are you conscious of German features in your work? Do you feel part of a German theatre tradition or of an international one?

I have never felt especially 'German' – I don't really know what that would be like. I think that's something to do with my education and my generation. German is my mother tongue, yes, and I am very fond of it, and of course there are links to the German narrative tradition – but *Peggy Pickit*, rather like *Push Up*, is essentially more 'English' in its conception. I had the basic idea for *The Animal Kingdom* in the canteen of the Royal Court Theatre. *Idomeneus* is an echo of ancient Greek theatre. I believe I feel more of a European ... and so the tradition I feel I belong to is a European or simply a theatrical one.

The questions were put by David Tushingham

*Jürgen Gosch (1943-2009) worked with Roland Schimmelpfennig for a number of years, directing the original productions of several Schimmelpfennig plays including *The Animal Kingdom*. His final production was *Idomeneus* which, at the time of writing, is still in repertoire at the Deutsches Theater, Berlin.

THE ANIMAL KINGDOM

The Animal Kingdom (*Das Reich der Tiere*) was given its world premiere at the Deutsches Theater Berlin on 1st September 2007 with the following cast:

Chris	Niklas Kohrt
Sandra/Antelope	Dörte Lyssewski
Dirk/Marabou	Wolfgang Michael
Frankie/Zebra	Falk Rockstroh
Peter/Lion	Ernst Stötzner
Isabel/Genet	Kathrin Wehlisch

Director: Jürgen Gosch

This translation of *Das Reich der Tiere* by Roland Schimmelpfennig was commissioned by The English Stage Company at the Royal Court Theatre.

Characters

PETER, actor, mid- to late thirties
In the animal kingdom THE LION
Later A FRIED EGG

DIRK, actor, over forty,
In the animal kingdom THE MARABOU
Later A SQUEEZY KETCHUP BOTTLE

ISABEL, actress, mid-thirties, younger than Peter
In the animal kingdom THE GENET
Later A PEPPERMILL

SANDRA, actress, mid- to late thirties,
In the animal kingdom THE ANTELOPE,
Later A PIECE OF TOAST

FRANKIE, actor, a little older than Peter,
In the animal kingdom THE ZEBRA

CHRIS, writer and director, early to mid-thirties.

A crocodile.

Maybe other animals: scorpions, giraffes, rhinoceroses,
elephants and others.

The animal costumes are original creations based on proper
ethnological research. Inspiration can be found in the works
of the indigenous peoples of North and South America, and of
Africa. Nothing cuddly or jokey. No-one walks or acts on four
legs. Fluid transformations from human to mythical or animal
form similar to many Egyptian or Aztec gods.

The footnotes are taken from the 1929 Leipzig Jubilee Edition
of *Brehm's Animal Life* edited by Carl W. Neumann and
published by Philipp Reclam jun.

Act One

1.

Two actors in their dressing room, PETER and FRANKIE. Both mid- to late thirties. FRANKIE is the older of the two. They have just come in and are still wearing their own clothes. FRANKIE has a large sports bag with him, which will be of significance later. They undress. Now they gradually transform themselves into animals: they put on make-up, paint their bodies, stick on hair or feathers or pieces of fur. By the end of the scene PETER will have turned into a LION, FRANKIE a ZEBRA. Both carry out a long and practised sequence of considered and skilful operations. Their movements are routine and in their assurance communicate something like pride or self-confidence. The quality and originality of both these (and the subsequent) animal costumes, combined with their simplicity, is very attractive. Towards the end of the scene they may also place expressive masks of wood, straw or paper on their heads, albeit without obscuring their faces.

PETER: *(Dismayed and irritated at the same time, disgusted.)*
A fried egg, – a fried egg?

FRANKIE:
Fried egg, yeah – a fried egg.

Pause.

PETER: *(Questioning, disgusted:)*
Or a bottle of ketchup?

Pause.

FRANKIE:
A fried egg and a bottle of ketchup –

PETER:
Ketchup. What is that – a fried egg and a ketchup bottle –

Brief pause. He's off again:

A piece of toast –

Brief pause.

A pepper pot –

Brief pause.

What's that supposed to be –

FRANKIE: *(Now equally irritated.)*
What's it supposed to be?

Brief pause.

What it is?

PETER:
What's it supposed to be –

Brief pause.

FRANKIE:
A fried egg.

Brief pause.

A bottle of ketchup. A piece of toast. Pepper.

Silence. Loud and abrupt:

PETER:
Oh yes!

Brief pause.

PETER:
Oh yes!

FRANKIE:
Yes!

Pause. Suddenly:

PETER:
A singing fried egg?
A talking fried egg?
Or a torturing pepper –

FRANKIE:

I dunno.

PETER:

Or a piece of dancing toast?

FRANKIE:

Maybe, yeah – I dunno.

PETER:

A bald egg. The fried egg's supposed to be bald.
They all are.

Brief pause.

There are limits.

FRANKIE:

Limits, yeah – .

PETER:

It's bollocks.

Suddenly:

FRANKIE:

You think about nothing else. Don't kid yourself, you think
about nothing else.

*Both continue transforming themselves the whole time. Sometimes
their quarrel is broken for longer periods because certain manoeuvres
require too much concentration to continue arguing with the required
force.*

*Whatever happens, the scene should last as long as it takes them both
to change into a zebra or a lion without any help from anyone else.*

PETER:

I'm not going to do it, I am not going to be a fried egg, I'm
not –

FRANKIE:

You think about nothing else.

PETER:

Me?

FRANKIE:

You –

PETER:

Me? Not me.

You, however:

He shouts:

You need that egg. Or the ketchup bottle.

Brief pause.

Nobody knows who you are.

FRANKIE:

I've been here longer than you. Everyone knows me.

PETER:

Exactly –

FRANKIE:

I've been here from the start –

PETER:

Exactly. You've been here from the start.

Brief pause.

You've been here six years.

Brief pause.

Six years.

Brief pause.

Six years!

Brief pause.

Six fucking years –

Brief pause.

Six years six days a week. Six days a week or more: every Christmas, every Easter.

Pause.

For six years. You are the zebra.

You've been the zebra for six fucking years.

FRANKIE carries on calmly with his make-up.

Nobody knows what you look like any more. You, rather than the zebra. Everyone knows the zebra. But none of them can remember you even exist.

2.

An antelope enters, a female. An oryx antelope[1], tall, slim, with horns that curve sharply upwards. The way she moves is wonderful, how she places one foot in front of another in high shoes, and how she stands there: proud, powerful, just standing there silently for a long time.

SANDRA:

I was the antelope for four years.

Pause.

---

1   Oryx antelopes have been known since ancient times and at least one species is depicted regularly on Egyptian and Nubian monuments. Here the oryx can be seen in a range of positions, usually with a cord around its neck as a sign that it has been hunted and captured. The same animal can be seen in the chambers of the pyramids of Cheops, often pictured with a single horn, which gave rise to the claim that the oryx had inspired the legend of the unicorn. According to Hartmann, the ancients depicted oryx antelopes with both straight and curved horns. This type were often kept tamed in ancient times and used in sacrifices. The oryx are among the largest and heaviest antelopes, however, they make a majestic impression despite their somewhat sturdy frames. The head is elongated without being misshapen, the facial lines almost straight or only a little curved, the neck mid-length, the body, which rests on relatively high strong limbs, is very strong, the tail is quite long with a heavy tuft at the tip. The eyes are large and expressive, the ears relatively short, wide and rounded. The horns, which are carried by both sexes, are very long and thin, ringed from the roots and are either straight or bent in a sweeping curve back and to the side.

(Brehm's Animal Life, Vol. 1, Mammals)

Then I got pregnant and had to drop out but now, after 10 months off, I'm back. I've only been out for 10 months.

Pause.

The baby's at my mum's most of the time.

She remains standing in the same position for some time. Then she strides off.

3.

ISABEL, mid-thirties, and DIRK, over forty. Both already partly in costume. She is busy turning herself into a genet[2], she paints her body, sticks things to it or puts on individual pieces of costume. Next to her, DIRK changes into a marabou[3] in the course of the scene.

Both complete their transformations via a series of well practised and scrupulously executed gestures, just as PETER and FRANKIE did.

ISABEL:

She didn't recognize me.

Brief pause.

Nobody knows what they're going to do. Nobody knows what's going to happen.

---

2   The genet *(viverra genetta)* inhabits Africa as far as Palestine and those areas of Europe bounding the Mediterranean. Its movements are as graceful and delicate as they are nimble and skilful. I know of no other mammal which can combine the flexibility of the snake with the speed of marten as it does. The manner in which it executes its movements cannot fail to inspire wonder. It seems to have a thousand joints. When it attacks, it glides across the ground, its slim body stretched out to form a straight line with its tail, the feet spread as wide apart as possible. Suddenly it leaps with one powerful bound onto its prey and catches it with infallible confidence.

    (Brehm's Animal Life, Vol. 2, Animals of Prey, Hunting Cats)

3   The ugliest of the storks is the marabou *(Leptoptilus crumeniferus)* with a crop-like pouch under its neck, a vast, powerful body, bare neck and bare head, covered at most with a few downy feathers, a massive beak, very thick at the root with a pointed, wedge-shaped tip, long legs, powerful wings and a mid-length tail whose lower feathers are strongly developed, slit from the roots and produce splendid ornamental feathers. Its head is flesh-coloured, its skin generally scabby, the plumage on its upper body is a dark metallic green, and that under its body and around its neck white.

DIRK:

They say they're not talking –

ISABEL:

Why's it called a 'Garden'? *The Garden of Things.* A fried egg, a bottle of ketchup. Why don't they call it 'The Abuse'.

Considers briefly.

Or 'The Torture'.

DIRK:

A piece of toast, didn't you say a piece of toast?

Brief pause.

Piece of toast, genet, marabou – it's all the same –

ISABEL:

Things –

She reaches for the mobile phone in front of her for a moment, looks at it:

D'you know how –

She changes the subject.

Or 'The Camp'.

DIRK:

At least now we know what's coming next.

ISABEL:

What's coming next –

DIRK:

What it's about –

ISABEL:

Do we? I don't know what it's about –

DIRK:

Aside from –

Brief pause.

Aside from –

ISABEL:

Aside from what?

DIRK:

Aside from who, aside from the question of who –

Brief pause.

Even if they're not –

Brief pause.

ISABEL:

I am not dressing up as a bottle of ketchup. I am not dressing up as a piece of toast. I'm not mental! I am not mental!

DIRK:

They say they're not talking, but they are talking, not to everyone, but talking is being done, that's the point. What's going to happen to them, to the ones they're not talking to –

ISABEL:

Yes, but –

Brief pause.

She didn't recognize me. What's the point of talking, she didn't even recognize me, what is the point of talking, she doesn't even know I work here.

What have you done in the last few years, she asked me.

How do you mean –

Well, what you've done in the last few years –

But you know me, you know my contract – you know what I've been doing for the last few years, the genet, that's what I've been doing for the last few years.

20

I would really like to know what's going to happen.
I don't know what's coming next!

FRANKIE and PETER. Forceful, loud, fast.

FRANKIE:
　Without me you'd –

PETER:
　Without me you'd –

FRANKIE:
　Without me you'd never have made it.

PETER:
　Without you I'd be –

FRANKIE:
　Without me you'd have been finished years ago –

PETER:
　There's a limit.

FRANKIE:
　A limit –

PETER:
　I've –

FRANKIE:
　What limit –

PETER:
　I –

FRANKIE:
　You wouldn't even 've –

PETER:
　I don't –

FRANKIE:

Not even a –

PETER:

I owe you nothing, nothing at all –

FRANKIE:

Nothing, you'd just be one big fat zero.

PETER:

I owe you nothing –

FRANKIE:

Without me, you'd be nothing and you'd be nowhere.

PETER:

You're not getting out of here.

Brief pause.

I've never understood what it is you want from me.

I owe you nothing, nothing at all –

FRANKIE:

You're not going to make it without me. Without me you're nothing.

4.2

Music. The animals enter: THE GENET, THE ANTELOPE, THE MARABOU, THE LION, THE ZEBRA.

THE GENET: From days of yore the zebra had been King of the animals, for the zebra is strong and fast and clever and unyielding.

No-one has ever ridden a zebra, no-one has ever succeeded in harnessing a zebra before a plough or carriage, no-one has ever been able to tame a zebra.

THE ANTELOPE: The zebra is free and not even the mosquitoes bite it because its black and white stripes confuse the midges, they cannot see the zebra, not even in the light of day. The zebra has never harmed another animal, for the zebra eats no meat, the zebra eats grass. This is how the zebra lived in the African steppes and ruled justly over the animals.

THE MARABOU: But then the lion, that fearsome hunter, demanded the crown because he was the strongest of the animals and had a claim on the throne from days of yore. This is what the lion shouted and his cry resounded across the steppes: I am the King, not the zebra –

THE LION: I am the King, not the zebra, I am the ruler of the animal kingdom, give me the crown.

THE GENET: For three days, his angry shouts could be heard at sunrise and sunset, the wind carried the lion's cries a long way across the steppes: the animals heard them, the antelope, the gazelle, the giraffe, the elephant, the rhinoceros, the scorpions, the spiders, the large and small birds, the genet, and they also reached the ears of the zebra.

THE MARABOU: The zebra summoned the marabou and told him to fly in circles over the grassy steppes calling all the animals in the kingdom together to a great assembly before sunset at the water hole: come to the great assembly of all the animals in the kingdom, where the animals themselves shall decide who is their ruler from now on: the zebra or the lion.

THE ANTELOPE: And so, as the shadows grew longer, the animals began to arrive at the water hole to hold their council. The antelope, the genet, the marabou, the zebra, the lion, the giraffe, the gazelle, the rhinoceros, the elephant and all the others.
A hot day is coming to an end. The rainy season is past. The grass stands tall on the steppes. Soon the sun will have set.

THE MARABOU: And then the Assembly began. Here sat the lion and there sat the zebra. There stood the great

23

elephant, the ancient privy councillor of the animal kingdom, and as soon as the last animal had taken its place, he began the proceedings: We have come together today to make a decision who should be our King.

The zebra has ruled us well for many years, now the lion demands the crown, because the lion, he says, is stronger than the zebra.

THE LION: That's right, shouted the lion. I demand the crown by right, I am the King of the animals.

Unrest. Small birds began chattering, everyone spoke in excitement and confusion, the humming birds and the bees and the mice.

THE MARABOU: Quiet, said the elephant, quiet.

Why should you become King, lion, because you are stronger than the zebra? A lot of animals are stronger than the zebra, and a lot of animals are stronger than you.

THE LION: What animal, show me the animal that's stronger than me, roared the lion.

THE MARABOU: The rhinoceros is stronger than you, countered the elephant, and the hippopotamus and I am too – and with that the elephant lowered his long tusks.

THE ANTELOPE: Yes, shouted the rhinoceros, I'm stronger than you, why can't I be our new King?

THE LION: Because I'm cleverer, shouted the lion.

THE MARABOU: You may be cleverer than the zebra, countered the elephant, but several animals are cleverer than the zebra: the hyena and the snake and the spider and the scorpion –

THE GENET: Yes, shouted the scorpion, I want to be King of the animals!

THE LION: You live in the shadow under a rock, called the lion, but I cut through the steppes with long strides.

THE GENET: So do I, shouted the flamingo bird.

THE ZEBRA: The zebra had remained silent up until now.
But now he spoke:
Yes, that's right. You do cut through our kingdom with
long strides – but your strides aren't as powerful as the
elephant's or as long as the giraffe's, although you do run
on powerful, dangerous paws.
But often you hide in the long grass. Often you creep
forward crouching, downwind, often you seek the cover
of night and then you're hunting, then you're looking for
meat and the only animal who's safe from you is the one
who can see you quick enough to escape, or else you'll kill
it with a single bite to the neck and feast on it. How do you
propose to be King of the animals if you're going to go
around hunting your own subjects?

THE ANTELOPE: Once again the small animals began to talk in
excitement and confusion, the humming birds and the bees
and the mice.

THE LION: And then the lion, the fearsome hunter, stood up
and said: maybe there are animals who are stronger than
I am. Maybe there are animals who are bigger than I am,
and some who are cleverer than I am.
But – and now his voice turned into a threatening growl
– I still demand the crown and sceptre because there is
no animal, whether it's big or strong or small or clever
or brightly coloured or black and white striped, that can
defeat me.

THE GENET: Suddenly the wind turns. The marabou takes
flight. The animals sense the danger immediately: and the
lion can sense it too.
Smoke. Fire. The steppes are burning. In the distance the
sky is already red with flames. No-one knows where to go.

The animals suddenly flee away from the fire.

PETER and DIRK

PETER:

Is she still here? I thought she wasn't here any more –

DIRK:

Didn't she leave? She left –

PETER:

Or – she did though – or she's come back again –

DIRK:

Come back? Maybe she has come back.

PETER:

But she'd gone. She had gone.

DIRK:

She had, yeah – Though that was her – wasn't it?
It might not have been her.

PETER:

It was her –

DIRK:

Then she's come back.

PETER:

If it was her.

DIRK:

You should know.

PETER:

Me?

DIRK:

You.

Brief pause.

She had a baby.

PETER:

I dunno.

DIRK:

She left to have a baby.

PETER:

I dunno.

DIRK:

And now she's come back. If it was her –

PETER:

Maybe. Maybe not. Hard to say.

DIRK:

Wasn't there something between you two? Weren't you together for a while?

PETER:

Before that. Didn't last long.

DIRK:

Well –

PETER:

But with those horns –

Brief pause.

Unrecognizable. With her face all – unrecognizable.

Brief pause.

But at the water hole I thought: judging by the arse: yeah, could well be.

Brief pause.

At the water hole, when she bent down to drink along with the others, I thought. Yep, that's her arse alright. Hello arse. That arse hasn't changed.

SANDRA, the female antelope, alone.

SANDRA:

I thought, after such a long time, after all those months, after more than ten months, I'd go through the building and say hello to people. Tell them how glad I am to be back. I'm really glad to be back.

Why, she asks me.

Why –

Why, did you go away, were you ill? I hadn't noticed –

She hadn't noticed I was gone. For ten months. More than ten months.

Brief pause.

And no-one asks about the baby.

Brief pause.

No-one asks about the baby. No-one asks what it is, a boy or a girl. And no-one asks what its name is.

7.

ISABEL and FRANKIE

FRANKIE:

Are you going to come to that thing after–

ISABEL: *(Removes bandage from her foot.)*
SSSSSSSsssssssssssssss

FRANKIE:

Hm?

ISABEL:

Can you have a look at that –

FRANKIE:

What?

ISABEL:

This bit here, please just look at it.

FRANKIE bends down to look at the area. FRANKIE recoils, it stinks.

FRANKIE:

What's wrong with your nail?

ISABEL:

What is wrong with my nail?

FRANKIE:

I'm asking you, what's wrong with it?

ISABEL:

I don't know, I've no idea – I don't know –

FRANKIE:

I can't see it –

ISABEL:

What do you mean?

FRANKIE:

I can't see the nail –

ISABEL:

Where is it then?

FRANKIE:

'T's not here –

ISABEL: *(Breathes in in pain.)*
Sssssss.

FRANKIE:

'T's not there. The nail's come off.

ISABEL: *(Breathes out in pain.)*
Haaaaahaaahhh.

FRANKIE: *(Picks up the bloody bandage and unwraps it. He holds the nail in his hand.)*
Here –

ISABEL: *(Breathes in in pain.)*
Ssssss.

Horror.

What's that?

FRANKIE:
The nail –

ISABEL:
My nail?

FRANKIE:
'S been torn off.

ISABEL:
Put it on. Put it back on again –

FRANKIE:
Where –

ISABEL:
On my toe.

FRANKIE:
That's not going to –

ISABEL:
Put it back on –

FRANKIE:
It's only going to hurt more –

ISABEL:
Do it, get on with it.

FRANKIE:
It's all exposed –

ISABEL:
That's why I'm telling you to put it back on again –

ISABEL grabs the nail and places it back on the spot where it used to be and bandages her foot up again. While she's doing this she deliberately lets out a series of short screams in an effort to manage the pain. She then limps off.

8.

Music. The animals: THE ANTELOPE, THE LION, THE ZEBRA, THE MARABOU, THE GENET.

THE ANTELOPE: The steppes are burning. The animals run but the fire is quicker, the wind drives the flames ever forward. The animal kingdom is on fire and the flames race across the steppes faster than the antelope or the genet can jump, faster than the marabou can fly, faster than the zebra, faster than the lion, the danger comes ever closer.

THE MARABOU: Then the animals reach a broad river. The smoke is already filling their lungs. Come on, come on, calls the marabou, who is already fluttering over the water, come on, and then the gazelle and the antelope crash into the water, the giraffe and the genet, the mice, the snakes and the scorpion, the rhinoceros and the elephant.

THE ZEBRA: Only the zebra stays behind on the bank, concerned and watchful that every one of the animals braves the jump into the rescuing waters – the spiders, the ostrich –

THE LION: And the lion stays behind, because, unlike the zebra, the lion, the wild animal, knows fear.
The lion is afraid of man's whip which can make him obey in the circus and the lion is afraid of the water, because he cannot swim.

THE ZEBRA: Jump on, the zebra shouts to the lion, to his worst enemy, I'll carry you to the other side. I'll swim with you to the other side –

THE LION: The lion roars at the flames –

THE ZEBRA: Jump on!

THE LION: The lion walks round in circles and roars and hisses and only when the tuft of his tail catches fire does he jump onto the zebra and the zebra swims with him across the river.

THE ZEBRA: The zebra tries to reach the other side of the river with the lion on his back. The eyes of the crocodile pop up above the surface of the water.

THE ANTELOPE: The crocodile, shouts the antelope, who, like the other animals, has already reached the other bank.

THE GENET: The crocodile, shouts the genet. The crocodile is less than two metres away from the zebra and the lion and it is already opening its deadly mouth.

9.

FRANKIE.

FRANKIE:

We said one time, when this job's finished, when it's all over – after such a long time – then we're going to do something totally different. When they close this down. When they chuck us out on the streets.

Then we'll think of something ourselves, our own story.

Without Peter I'd never have had the idea – but Peter wouldn't have had it without me either.

It's a really simple idea:

Two men, actors, lose their jobs.

And they can't get new ones. They apply. Send off letters, photos, CVs. One of them uses the last money he's got to buy a ticket to a gala benefit, so he can make contacts with the right kind of people. It doesn't work. There are no jobs.

The only jobs there are are for women.

So these two unemployed actors dress up as women. They
end up with a cleaning company which puts them both
in a cleaning team. There's a Turkish woman, a Bolivian,
a Polish woman, a German and an Italian. None of these
women speak the same language. And they're joined by
these two men: one pretends he's Lebanese, the other one
Iranian. Both of them wear headscarves. They talk in this
made-up Arabic.

A load of women and two guys in drag.

10.

DIRK and SANDRA.

SANDRA:
    Are you going along later to the –

DIRK: *(Sighs.)*
    Can you look, can you please look and see what that is –

SANDRA:
    What?

DIRK:
    It hurts, there's something hurting there, aaah –

SANDRA:
    Where?

DIRK:
    Here, here, there –

SANDRA: *(Inspects a wound in DIRK's neck.)*
    Oh –

DIRK:
    What –

SANDRA: *(Only now fully realising how deep the injury is.)*
    Auhhh –

DIRK:

What is it –

SANDRA: *(Medically pessimistic.)*

Mmh

DIRK:

What is there –

SANDRA:

Looks bad.

DIRK:

What's there?

SANDRA:

Ooh, that does not look good.

DIRK:

Aaah –

SANDRA:

God, that looks bad.

DIRK:

It really stings.

SANDRA:

The skin's broken. It's infected.

DIRK:

Where?

SANDRA:

Here, underneath the feathers. 'S all infected.

DIRK:

Oh no –

SANDRA: *(Poking around in the wound.)*

'S a real hole. There's a real hole in the skin. How can that –

DIRK:

The feathers get stuck on and then torn off. Keep being

torn off. And then stuck on again. I've had a rash there for
years –

SANDRA:

Leave them on.

DIRK:

I can't go around in the street like that. With feathers on
my neck.

11.

Brief music.

The animals.

THE ZEBRA is carrying THE LION through the river.

THE CROCODILE is getting closer.

12.

ISABEL.

ISABEL:

An egg, a fried egg, that's bald. Together with a bottle
of ketchup, a pepper mill, a slice of toast, all bald, silent,
standing facing each other. Are these objects, or are
they prisoners? What is this, the world's silence? The
nothingness of breakfast? The struggle for survival?
They stand facing each other, silent, massive, then they
each bow down, they abase themselves. That's a stage
direction. An important clue – but what does it mean?

13.

*Brief music. The animals: THE MARABOU, THE LION, THE ZEBRA, THE
ANTELOPE, THE GENET.*

THE MARABOU: The crocodile opens its deadly, insatiable jaws,
it's already reached the zebra and the lion and its long
tail is beating the water in its excitement and bloodthirsty

anticipation when the lion strikes the crocodile dead with a single blow of its paw. The crocodile's body sinks down onto the riverbed, dead.

THE LION: Without me the crocodile would have eaten you, says the lion, once he's reached the opposite bank on the zebra's back.

THE ZEBRA: Without me you'd have perished, you'd have been burnt alive, replies the zebra.

THE LION AND THE ZEBRA: When the zebra and the lion jumped into the river, they were allies bound together by a common danger, but when they arrived at the far shore, they were enemies.

THE ANTELOPE: There were animals who now said that the zebra was the King of the animals because without the zebra the lion would have burnt or drowned in the river.

THE GENET: But there were also other animals who said that without the lion, the zebra would have been torn to pieces by the crocodile and that only one animal could have defeated the crocodile and that therefore from now on the lion had to be king of the animals.

THE ANTELOPE: But if the zebra hadn't carried the lion through the water –

THE MARABOU: But if the lion hadn't killed the crocodile –

14.

ISABEL and PETER.

PETER:
No. *The Garden of Things.* No.

ISABEL:
Go. Listen to it.

PETER:
No.

ISABEL:

Frankie's going.

PETER:

Frankie, yeah, Frankie, you know what, Frankie's got shit
for brains, so he ought to go and listen to that shit, I'm not
listening to it. I'm not going.

15.

FRANKIE alone.

FRANKIE:

Without me he'd never've had the idea about the women.
The cleaners with these two unemployed actors start work
at 4.30 every morning, cleaning an enormous bank. A
tower of glass in the morning gloom.
There are all kinds of really funny situations, especially
with the other women, in this made-up Arabic.

16.

Brief music. The animals.

THE LION: The animals had formed two groups. One group
admired the strength of the lion and they swore to be
his subjects: the leopard was one of them, the puma, the
panther, the jaguar, the genet, and also the scorpion and
the snake, the termites, the spider, the hyena and the
eagles.

THE ZEBRA: The others feared the strength of the lion and his
teeth and therefore they stood with the zebra: the elephant,
the rhinoceros, the antelope, the giraffe and they were
joined by the gazelle and the bees.
Only the marabou, the stork of the steppes, flew agitatedly
from one group to the other.

THE GENET: What now? The sun set. The animals lay down to
sleep.

THE LION: But that night the lion walked about silently between the sleeping animals.

THE ANTELOPE: The antelope awoke in the middle of the night because she could feel the warm breath of the lion on her neck. What do you want from me?

THE LION: And the lion whispered: I worship your beauty, I love you, I've loved you for a long time, and when I am King of the animals, you shall be my Queen, the Queen of the animals.

THE ANTELOPE: That pleased the antelope.

17.

PETER, DIRK

PETER:

The men have spent a long time planning how to rob the bank they clean every morning. Eventually while they're supposed to be cleaning the leather armchairs on the executive floor they transfer a hundred million dollars by an untraceable route to a Swiss account.

Of course the other women, the Bolivian, the Vietnamese, the Pole and so on have all been in it for ages – this all comes out at some point in a surprising twist – and when the women eventually reach Switzerland by rowing a boat across Lake Constance, they all dress up as businessmen. In the last scene we see them all in pinstripe suits and they've all got stubble, sunglasses and short haircuts. Their ties are flapping in the wind. And you're there, as a man who's disguised as a woman who's disguised as a man, behind the wheel of this massive motor boat on Lake Constance on the way to freedom.

DIRK:

But it was Frankie's idea –

PETER:

Frankie? Why Frankie? Why's it Frankie's idea –

DIRK:

Didn't you develop the idea with Frankie?

PETER:

Yeah but it's not Frankie's idea. It's my idea. And it's your idea too, that bit with the suits and the ties that's your idea –

18.

Brief music, the animals.

THE MARABOU: That night, when all the animals were asleep, the lion went to the marabou and woke him with the following words:

THE LION: Of all the animals, you are the most learned. You have no dangerous claws and no sharp teeth, but you have a large beak, you are perceptive and clever. When I am the King of the animals, you shall be my deputy. You shall take the place of the zebra and use your intelligence to steer the fate of the nation and only one animal shall stand above you: I, the lion. That pleased the marabou, who had long dreamed of being more than a stork.

THE GENET: And that night the lion also went to the genet and said the following words in her ear:
My distant cousin, my delicate little sister, tiny cat, let us be something other than what we have to be.

THE LION: Let us forget what we are and become something different. We want to break out, to transform ourselves, to be free. When I am King of the animals, we want to live without boundaries, without need and without force and everyone may grow beyond themselves, every one may be what they would most like to be.

THE ANTELOPE: And so in the course of that night the lion named the elephant his historian, he made the termites his construction engineers, he named the humming birds his reporters, the giraffe together with the scorpion became his secret service and he named the rhinoceros his grenadier.

THE ZEBRA: The next morning the animals chose the lion to be their King and the new King began the first day of his rule by hunting.

He hunted the zebra.

THE LION: But the zebra was quicker than the lion. He may have been hot on the zebra's heels but he could not catch it. Finally he paused exhausted and the zebra too stood still at a safe distance. Then the lion tried to kill the zebra again but once again he couldn't catch it. And so they went further and further away from the river and the steppe and the other animals until they reached the foot of a high mountain.

THE ZEBRA: And the lion kept on hunting the zebra, on and on they climbed higher and higher, the mountain was rugged, rocky, bare and steep and full of dangerous crevices and abysses, soon it began to snow, snow was something neither of the animals had ever known until then and they were unfamiliar with its dangers. A storm arose, a snow storm in which it snowed so much they couldn't see anything any more and that is how it happened that the zebra, climbing ever higher, lost its footing, slipped, plunged into a deep gorge and died.

THE LION: The lion, however, got lost in the storm and for several days was unable to find the way back to his kingdom. Then when he did finally find his home again, he had changed, he was no longer the same.

It was as if he was now the hunted one, the quarry.

Because even if he didn't want to believe it, and he never told a word of it to anyone, he often thought he saw the zebra's ghost, running right in front of him, almost reachable with a single bound, a ghost he was compelled to follow without ever being able to catch.

PETER, DIRK, SANDRA, ISABEL and FRANKIE. They might be wearing dressing gowns over the top of their costumes.

PETER:

    Six years.

    Pause. PETER looks around the group.

    Six whole years.

    Pause.

    I mean six, SIX fucking years.

    He doesn't take his eyes off DIRK and SANDRA, in order to see the effect he's hoping for in their faces.

    Can you imagine? SIX years. Six poxy fucking years.

    Pause.

    Six!

    Pause.

    Every day for six years.

    Brief pause. To FRANKIE:

    I mean how do you justify that to yourself?

    Brief pause.

    We keep hearing, they're not talking.

    Brief pause.

    But of course they're talking.
    There are offers.

    Brief pause.

DIRK:

    I know they're talking. I know.

Brief pause.

You know it, I know it, they've probably been talking to you for ages. And to you – and to you. Haven't they? No-one says they're talking. No-one. But everyone's probably been talking for ages. Everyone. Except me.

Brief pause.

They're not talking to me –

Brief pause. PETER *laughs out loud.*

DIRK:

They might, but not yet, I keep thinking they don't even know who I am, what I look like, when they see me in the corridor they probably think I work in the accounts department.

Brief pause.

PETER:

Maybe it'll happen.

ISABEL:

Paradise Lost, the Fallen Angel – the battle of the angels, the war between good and evil –

Heaven and Hell: you can make something out of that.

The Battle of the Angels: it's better than a bunch of cleaners and men in drag.

DIRK:

The egg! They've offered you the egg! Haven't they? Haven't they?

Act Two

1

The flat of a single man between thirty and forty. Night. No-one there. A key can be heard in the lock. The front door opens. FRANKIE and CHRIS. Both are roughly the same age. FRANKIE has a large sports bag with him.

FRANKIE: *(Turns the light on.)*
    Come in.

CHRIS:
    Thanks.

FRANKIE:
    Here – here's the phone.

CHRIS:
    Where's the phone –

FRANKIE:
    Here.

FRANKIE: *(Passes him a somewhat outdated phone on a cord.)*

CHRIS: *(Picks up the receiver but does not dial.)*

FRANKIE: *(After a brief moment.)*
    Who – who are you going to call now –

CHRIS:
    I don't know – someone at the theatre, the secretary, the assistant, the woman from the press office –

Brief pause. He doesn't have the number.

FRANKIE:
    Have you got the number?

CHRIS:
    No I haven't got the number, how am I supposed to have the number, haven't you got the number?

FRANKIE:

No, I haven't got the number –

CHRIS:

You've not got the number?

Brief pause.

You haven't got the assistant's number?

FRANKIE:

No –

CHRIS:

You haven't?

FRANKIE:

No.

CHRIS:

But you've got the secretary's number –

FRANKIE:

No, I'm sorry –

CHRIS:

Why not, I thought you worked there –

FRANKIE:

Yes, I did work there, I still do work there, but only
– I haven't got the numbers –

CHRIS:

You must have the numbers –

FRANKIE:

I haven't got the numbers, I always call the switchboard –

CHRIS:

The switchboard – then call the switchboard –

Tries to pass him the phone. FRANKIE *doesn't take it.*

Please –

FRANKIE:

There's no-one there now –

CHRIS:

Now?!

FRANKIE:

It's almost half twelve –

CHRIS:

Isn't there, isn't there like a list, usually the theatre's
got some kind of list, with all the names on, the phone
numbers, everywhere I work, there's always a list, in every
city – in every theatre, there has never not been some kind
of list, even in –

FRANKIE:

Sorry, I'm sorry, I don't have a list –

CHRIS: *(Desperate.)*

I don't believe this. No list.

Brief pause.

FRANKIE:

Maybe.

CHRIS:

I don't believe it.

FRANKIE:

Maybe there is a list like that –

CHRIS:

I thought there wasn't a list –

FRANKIE:

Maybe there is but I never got one –

CHRIS: *(Easily hopeful.)*

Maybe you have got a list but you forgot about it.
Have a look –

FRANKIE:

Haven't you got the numbers, didn't they give you the numbers –

CHRIS:

Course.

Pause.

Course. They gave me everything. The numbers, the assistant's number, the press woman's number, the name of the hotel, the phone number for the hotel, the address for the hotel, everything – everything.

FRANKIE:

So what was the name of the hotel –

CHRIS:

I dunno, I've already told you, if I knew the name of the hotel I wouldn't be here – it was on the sheet – it was all on the sheet –

FRANKIE:

And you're sure that that sheet –

CHRIS:

The sheet was in my rucksack. In my wallet.

Pause.

I just don't understand it –

FRANKIE:

The rucksack was by the table, next to the microphone –

CHRIS:

Yeah –

FRANKIE:

I noticed that, I wondered if you always do that, why do you do that, why do you take your rucksack on stage with you – why don't you leave it in the dressing room?

CHRIS:

> I don't leave my stuff in the dressing room because if it's
> left in the dressing room it gets nicked –

> *Brief pause.*

> 'T's all gone. Everything. Phone. Cash. Credit cards.

> *Brief pause.*

> The phone. – Oh Christ. Jesus.

> *Brief pause.*

> My agent was going to call me again at one about that –

> *Brief pause.*

> If only I'd noticed it earlier – if I'd noticed a bit earlier –
> suddenly everyone had gone –

> *Brief pause.*

> If you hadn't come and talked to me, I'd have been
> completely lost.

> *Brief pause.*

> Address book, diary, keys. Tickets. I've got nothing left.

> *Pause. Suddenly it occurs to him –*

> I'm not going to be able to leave, tomorrow I've got to –
> tomorrow morning I've got to go on to –

FRANKIE:

> Where? Where've you got to go tomorrow morning?

CHRIS:

> It was on the sheet –

FRANKIE:

> On the sheet?

47

CHRIS:

On the other sheet, the sheet with the appearances, on the print-out from –

Brief pause. He looks at FRANKIE *questioningly –*

Malmö? Didn't I say something about Malmö before?

FRANKIE:

Malmö? I don't know, you talked about Stockholm and New York, you talked about your own project, that you're going to finance that by filming the ad in New York, the ad with the puddle and the man carrying the woman, even though you don't normally do films and definitely not ads and definitely not copies of some idea ripped off from somewhere else, but this time – because of the project –

CHRIS:

There was something in Scandanavia – Oslo?

PETER:

Could be, Oslo, but you didn't say anything about Scandanavia, just the opera in Milan and the opera in Hamburg.

Long pause.

CHRIS: *(Incredulous.)*

I don't believe this.

Brief pause.

I do not believe this.

Brief pause.

I don't believe it.

Pause.

In front of my eyes. In front of everyone's eyes. The thing was right next to me the whole time. I just cannot believe it.

Brief pause. He has an idea.

But it's all online, they sent me it, all the numbers, the list –

He is as if redeemed.

I hope I've still got it, I hope I didn't delete it – can I use your computer for a minute, I just need to use your computer –

Brief pause.

Then I'll be out of here –

FRANKIE:
Oh –

CHRIS:
What is it –

FRANKIE:
You need the computer –

CHRIS:
Everything's online. Two minutes and I'll be out of here –

FRANKIE:
But the computer –

CHRIS:
What about the computer.

FRANKIE:
The computer's ancient.

CHRIS:
Doesn't matter.

FRANKIE:
The computer won't boot up.

CHRIS:
It won't boot up?

FRANKIE:
No –

Brief pause.

CHRIS:

Can I have a look at it?

Brief pause.

Can I have a look at it?

2.

THE MARABOU.

THE MARABOU: The marabou is an animal which, despite its
size, lives in constant fear. Some people say it swaggers.
Maybe. But that's because it has to cross uncertain ground.
Because its feet can hardly support it. The marabou has
the largest wingspan of any bird apart from the Chilean
condor, bigger than an eagle. It's a bird with giant wings.
But it's no hunter. The marabou feeds off carrion. And as
a result he doesn't know where he belongs. He gnaws the
rotting bones other animals have left behind.

3.

At FRANKIE's. The same night. CHRIS and FRANKIE.

CHRIS:

The computer's dead. Completely dead.

CHRIS listens to the computer. Pause.

FRANKIE:

Can't you ring someone up to look online for you?
A friend?

Brief pause.

CHRIS:

How?

FRANKIE:

With a phone. Here, with my phone.

CHRIS:

But I haven't got the number.

Brief pause.

The numbers are all in my phone. Or in my address book. My address book's in the hotel. I don't know where the hotel is. I don't know the hotel's name.

FRANKIE:

Can't you remember one number.

CHRIS:

No.

FRANKIE:

Any number –

CHRIS:

No!

FRANKIE:

Any number of anybody who's particularly close to you –

CHRIS:

No.

FRANKIE:

No-one?

CHRIS:

No.

Brief pause.

Don't you know someone you can ring up.

FRANKIE:

Me?

Brief pause.

Now?

CHRIS:

Yes, now – maybe. Someone who can then use their computer – for me – to go –

Brief pause.

FRANKIE:

Sure. I should have thought of that earlier –

He takes the phone and dials a number from memory. He waits.

No-one there.

He carries on waiting. Then hangs up.

'S no-one there – wait.

He dials another number, waits – hangs up.

Sorry.

Silence. CHRIS throws himself onto the sofa or some other form of chair. Great pose as victim of life's conspiracies; 'if life is going to treat me like this then it really doesn't deserve me.'

CHRIS:

No. no. No no no. No no no no no.

CHRIS finds something in his trouser pocket – happy, surprised.

CHRIS:

Hey – look at this –

He holds up a smooth and entirely white plastic card.

FRANKIE:

What's that?

CHRIS:

It's my key –

FRANKIE:

What key –

CHRIS: *(Incredibly excited.)*

My hotel key –

Brief pause.

FRANKIE:

Hey, that's great, what's it say on it –

CHRIS: *(Looks at the key.)*

FRANKIE:

Which hotel is it?

Brief pause.

What's the matter –

CHRIS:

There's no name on it –

FRANKIE:

What?

CHRIS:

There's no name on it. Nothing. No name, no address. Not even the room number – there's nothing on it at all!

Brief pause.

Why? Why?

Brief pause.

I'm not going to get out of here.

FRANKIE: *(Friendly.)*

You don't have to get out of here.

CHRIS: *(Shouts.)*

I do, you don't understand, I've got to get out of here. I've GOT to get out of here.

Brief pause.

FRANKIE:

Ok, ok –

Brief pause.

CHRIS:

> Thanks for letting me come here – if you hadn't let me
> come here, then –

FRANKIE:

> That's fine. No worries.

> *Brief pause.*

> You can sleep here. You're welcome. No worries.
> D'you want a drink –

> *He fetches something to drink and two glasses. Pause.*

CHRIS:

> What's your name?

FRANKIE:

> Frankie.

> *Long pause.*

CHRIS:

> And you work at the theatre –

FRANKIE:

> Yeah –

CHRIS:

> What do you do?

FRANKIE:

> I'm an actor.

CHRIS:

> So what did do last?

FRANKIE:

> A play called: In *The Animal Kingdom.*

CHRIS: *(Incredulous.)*

> But I saw that. Today, before the reading, they got me a
> ticket – I didn't recognize you. I'm sorry, I didn't recognize
> you at all.

Pause.

So who were you –

CHRIS:

FRANKIE:

It's not that important –

CHRIS:

Come on, tell –

FRANKIE:

I was the zebra –

CHRIS:

Which zebra, there were a couple of zebras –

FRANKIE:

There are three zebras, I mean the zebra that fights the lion
at the end –

CHRIS:

The one – the one who's betrayed by his friend –

FRANKIE:

Yeah –

CHRIS:

The zebra –

FRANKIE:

The part's not actually called the zebra, the character's
called Flip.

CHRIS:

That's the lead.

FRANKIE:

One of the leads.

CHRIS:

The zebra and the lion, they're the leads – who plays the
lion again –

FRANKIE:

A friend of mine.

CHRIS:

You were better. You moved better. Your voice.

Pleasantly surprised, apparently appreciative.

Really good songs. Well sung –

Brief pause.

CHRIS:

Good make-up. They were all good costumes. Amazing.

Pause.

How can you stand it?

FRANKIE:

A lot of people ask that.

Brief pause.

'S ok though.

Pause.

CHRIS:

How long's the show been going?

FRANKIE:

Six years.

CHRIS:

Six years!

Brief pause.

But not with the same cast.

FRANKIE:

Some of them.

CHRIS:

And how long have you been in it?

FRANKIE:

From the beginning.

CHRIS:

No!

FRANKIE:

Yes!

CHRIS:

Six years! Six years of being the zebra.

FRANKIE:

Yeah.

CHRIS:

What about the others?

FRANKIE:

Depends. Isabel, the genet, 's been doing it for four years.

CHRIS:

The genet – I thought that was meant to be an antelope.

FRANKIE:

The antelope's the other one, the tall one, the one with
the –

CHRIS:

What do you call those animals with the long horns –

FRANKIE:

That's the antelope.

CHRIS:

So which one was the genet –

FRANKIE:

The wiry one who can move really fast –

CHRIS:

Oh yeah –

FRANKIE:

Dirk, the marabou,'s been there from the beginning like
me. But he didn't start as the marabou.

CHRIS:

Nice idea: the educated middle classes represented by a bird, ridden with anxiety, devoid of character.

FRANKIE:

He started as one of the humming birds. Worked his way up.

Peter's only been there two years, I suggested it, told him he should audition – the guy who had the part before him did his cruciate ligament on stage. Crack.

CHRIS:

Who's Peter?

FRANKIE:

Oh yeah. Peter's the lion.

Brief pause.

CHRIS:

How many performances a week is it?

FRANKIE:

Six. Seven. Sometimes nine.

CHRIS:

Tough.

Brief pause.

That is tough.

FRANKIE:

But not for much longer.

CHRIS:

How come?

FRANKIE:

They're taking it off.

CHRIS:

Oh right – course.

Brief pause.

And then?

FRANKIE:

Haven't a clue. I've been told they aren't talking but they are talking.

CHRIS:

Why don't you do your own thing. Get a couple of people together.

Make some contacts. Reinvent yourselves.

He stands up.

I'm just going to er –

FRANKIE:

That way.

CHRIS exits. FRANKIE alone. Suddenly a phone rings inside FRANKIE'S sports bag. FRANKIE leaps up, pulls a rucksack out of the sports bag at lightning speed, opens the rucksack, looks for the ringing phone, eventually finds it, tries to stop it ringing, this does not succeed immediately, finally he hits the phone against something and hides both the mobile and the rucksack underneath the sofa. CHRIS comes back.

CHRIS:

Nice flat. Was there a phone ringing just then?

FRANKIE:

Here?

CHRIS:

I thought I –

He's amused at his apparent hallucination.

I just thought I could hear my own phone. Like my phone was here in this flat.

Laughs.

FRANKIE:

Yeah. I nicked it, it's there in my bag.

He points to the bag.

I really got you there.

He pours out spirits and gives CHRIS a glass.

And all just to make some kind of connection with you.
You'd never have thought.

CHRIS:

Yes, yes –

FRANKIE:

Be right back.

FRANKIE exits. CHRIS alone with his glass. He stands around, undecided, looks around, then trawls rapidly through FRANKIE's sports bag without finding anything, closes it again. FRANKIE comes back.

FRANKIE:

I thought you were going to read from *The Garden of Things*.

CHRIS:

People aren't going to understand that in a reading, it's
something people have got to see, not hear.

FRANKIE:

The fried egg.

Brief pause.

How are we supposed to imagine something like: a human
pepper mill, bald.

CHRIS:

It's not about fried eggs. Or aluminium fish slices.

Brief pause.

It's about the situation. What happens there. What they do.

FRANKIE:

What the fried egg and the piece of toast do. And the
ketchup.

4

PETER.

PETER:

I'm only doing it if Frankie's not in it.

The way I see it Frankie is cowardice and boredom personified.

What do you mean if Frankie's not in it.

I'm only going to accept the Egg if Frankie's not in it.

But without Frankie –

Without Frankie!

Frankie's got to – Frankie's –

Fuck Frankie, I'm only doing it without Frankie –

You're going to do it, you're going to do the Fried Egg, but you'll only do it without Frankie.

Fuck Frankie, I'm only going to do it without Frankie.

5.

At FRANKIE's that same night. CHRIS and FRANKIE.

CHRIS:

A garden of failure and torture.

Long pause.

It's basically like your animal play. A parable of decline.

FRANKIE:

Is that the way you see it?

Brief pause.

FRANKIE:

I think I just didn't understand *The Garden of Things* –

CHRIS:

I think there are a lot of people who've not understood it – maybe it's impossible to understand it. Perhaps that's not what it's about.

Brief pause.

Presumably that's why I got The Theatre Prize for it too –

FRANKIE:

Oh did you? Awesome –

CHRIS:

Yeah, probably nobody really understood any of it but they all thought they had to understand it so to avoid having to admit they hadn't understood it, they gave me the prize.

FRANKIE:

Congratulations: The Theatre Prize. Well done.
That's awesome.

CHRIS:

Yeah yeah, but if you look at who's won that prize and who's never won it, then –

FRANKIE:

Doesn't matter, it's still awesome –

CHRIS:

Yeah, maybe –

Brief pause.

But I'm not going to accept the prize.

FRANKIE:

What?

CHRIS:

No, I won't accept it –

FRANKIE:

'S a lot of money –

CHRIS:

I don't mind the money, but – but I'm not going to take the prize. Jensen was on the jury.

FRANKIE:

Jensen? Who's Jensen?

CHRIS:

You don't need to know.

Brief pause.

He's a – . I'm not taking any prizes from Jensen.

Lengthy pause. Long enough for a change of subject.

And you don't know what you're going to do next.
When they take the animal play off. After six years,
you don't know what you're going to do next.

6.

THE ANTELOPE.

THE ANTELOPE: The antelope seems to live in peace, but the
truth is when she's grazing with her herd on the vast
expanses of the steppes she lives in constant fear, because
many animals are out hunting to kill her, this majestic
creature, she is continually being hunted, she spends every
moment of her life in danger.

Now, however, she will be Queen of the animals and she
will have nothing more to fear, never again, perhaps, and
yet she's still afraid, because she still does not know what
awaits her, what it will feel like: the kiss of the lion.

THE LION and THE ANTELOPE kiss.

7.

At FRANKIE's, that same night. FRANKIE and CHRIS.

CHRIS:

There's practically no difference between you and me.

He demonstrates this tiny difference with a gesture.

That much, maybe.

FRANKIE:

No. no, that's not right, that's just not right – you are definitely –

CHRIS:

>0.1 percent of our genetic material is what distinguishes humans from chimpanzees or something like that.
>
>And us: you and me, the difference between us is nothing, we're even the same age – 0.1 per cent chance – or luck – that's all, if I hadn't by chance met the right people –

FRANKIE:

>Yes, but that's not purely chance, you also need –

CHRIS:

>No, no,

FRANKIE:

>Yes you do –

CHRIS:

>Just the ideas – the idea –

FRANKIE:

>The ideas, yeah, right –
>
>*Brief pause.*

FRANKIE:

>And you had your company, your people, people who've all got careers now –

CHRIS:

>Hang on, I've always said that: make yourselves independent. Start your own company. Create networks. Networks make all the difference.

FRANKIE:

>I haven't got a network.

CHRIS:

>Then build one.
>
>*Pause.*

FRANKIE:

>Why can't I be part of your network –

Brief pause.

CHRIS: *(Laughing, amazed, and also rejecting.)*
    Hey – why should you be part of my network, I don't even
    know you.

FRANKIE:
    Six years.

Brief pause.

They always say they're not talking but they are talking.

Brief pause.

Do you know whether they're talking –

Brief pause.

Or can't you talk about that. You can't talk about that, can
you?

Brief pause.

I keep feeling that the conversation always starts in the
same place, you meet and you talk but there's never any
progress. There are no agreements, no rejections. Instead
the conversation just goes on over and over again from
the same place you started. There are pleasantries. Long
digressions about things that have got nothing to do with
me. Kenya. Schnitzler. Speyer. Goethe's father.

CHRIS:
    Have you asked yourself why that is – ?

FRANKIE:
    I'm not sure whether they'd even recognize me in the
    corridor. I'm not even sure they recognize me when I'm
    sitting in their office right in front of them. It happens. That
    has actually happened. They've said to someone sorry
    they're not taking anyone on who's already under contract
    to them and has been for years. Can you imagine that –
    can you imagine!

CHRIS:

I can tell you why that is: they're not really interested.

Brief pause.

It may be that they are talking to certain people, – but only because they can't find anyone else. No-one who'll do it –

FRANKIE:

I'd do it – I want to do it, I'd like nothing more!

Pause.

CHRIS:

Maybe you're just not good enough.

Pause. Before FRANKIE can say something –

Maybe you're just not good enough. A lot of actors have got this problem, they're just not good enough.

Brief pause.

And nobody tells them. For years.

Brief pause.

You're helping me. If it hadn't been for you, I'd have been completely lost.

FRANKIE:

You don't owe me anything –

CHRIS:

I'm not going to lie to you, which I certainly would have done otherwise, simply to avoid this situation: you just weren't particularly good. You weren't appalling bad, but you were not especially good either.

Brief pause.

I'm surprised they've kept you on here for six years.

Brief pause.

But I'm not surprised that you haven't found anything else in recent years.

People look at you and then they're not looking at you.

Brief pause.

There are actors who've got a kind of criminal intensity that you can sense instantly. That's just there. Who don't ask. Who just take what they need without thinking.

Brief pause.

Too little. Too shallow. Too boring. Not enough. Limited.

Pause.

You going to throw me out now? I'm telling you like it is. If you want I'll go now. If you want, you can throw me out.

Brief pause.

FRANKIE:

You've forgotten my name, haven't you? When you leave here tomorrow, you won't even know who I was.

Brief pause.

CHRIS:

'S true.

FRANKIE:

Have you –

Brief pause.

Here: I'll write it down for you. I'm going to write down my name and address and my phone number. I'm going to write it on this piece of paper.

Brief pause.

Don't lose that bit of paper. Keep it. Don't throw it away. Do not lose that piece of paper.

Act Three

1

PETER and SANDRA in their animal costumes as the LION and ANTELOPE as before. Some distance between them. Completely out of breath. We don't know why.

SANDRA:

The baby –

They are both breathing heavily, completely out of breath.

The baby –

Out of breath again.

The baby's yours.

Out of breath again.

Don't you want to know its name?

Brief pause.

Don't you want to know what it is?

Brief pause.

It's a boy.

Brief pause.

I'm not going to tell him you're the father.

Brief pause.

I'm going to tell him his father's dead!

2.

Brief music. THE GENET.

GENET: The animal kingdom changed after the zebra
disappeared, it fell apart. It had a ruler but that ruler did
not govern. He was pursued by a shadow that never let
him go. And so from now on the animal kingdom was
governed by futility and bloodlust.

3.

SANDRA, DIRK, ISABEL in their animal costumes.

SANDRA:

Did anyone go to the reading?

No answer.

He went to it.

Brief pause.

He went.

Brief pause.

Nobody else did. Did they? I didn't go to it, did you go?
I didn't go.

Brief pause.

'Course not.

Long pause. She adjusts some detail of her costume.

Gave him his number. Just wrote a few numbers on a piece
of paper. That was all. A bit of ink, a few numbers.

Brief pause.

It's worth a ton of money. An absolute ton of money.

Brief pause.

ISABEL:

    500 Euros.

DIRK:

    500 Euros.

ISABEL:

    'S a lot.

DIRK:

    Yeah, 's a lot.

    Brief pause.

DIRK:

    But –

    Brief pause.

ISABEL:

    500 Euros for a dinner.

DIRK:

    'S a benefit. A gala. Everyone's going to be there.

SANDRA:

    Who?

DIRK:

    People –

SANDRA:

    Have you got 500?

DIRK:

    No!

SANDRA:

    Right –

DIRK:

    But maybe you can get to know someone there –

ISABEL:

    Who?

DIRK:

I don't know.

Brief pause.

Enter PETER, he is completely incensed.

PETER:

Why – why –
why Frankie?

Brief pause. He still can't understand it.

Frankie?

DIRK:

Yeah, Frankie –

PETER:

Frankie's gone? Gone? To New York? Why New York?

DIRK:

I dunno, he's got some –

PETER:

He doesn't even look like –

DIRK:

He's got this –

PETER:

He doesn't look like –

DIRK:

He said he's got to carry a woman across a puddle in New York.

Brief pause.

PETER:

And the zebra?

DIRK:

I dunno –

PETER:

What's going to happen to the zebra –

DIRK:

The zebra's been cut –

PETER:

Without the zebra –

DIRK:

A new zebra –

PETER:

There's got to be a new zebra –

DIRK:

It's not worth getting a new zebra any more.

PETER:

That's –

He wants to say something but is incapable of speech.

PETER: *(Controlled, slowly.)*

So who's going to do what the zebra used to do now?

DIRK:

I am.

PETER:

You?

Brief pause.

But you – but you're –

DIRK:

There is no zebra any more –

PETER:

But you're not a zebra. You're a bird. The zebra's
important, how's the lion going to get across the river –

DIRK:

With me –

PETER:

You're going to carry me – the marabou –

DIRK:

'S a symbol.

Brief pause.

And you kill the crocodile –

PETER:

But you're too – how's the marabou going to get the lion, I mean, the marabou can't replace the zebra, nobody's going to believe that –

Brief pause.

Nobody is going to believe that!

4.

Brief music.

THE MARABOU carries THE LION through the river.

A CROCODILE comes closer and opens its jaws.

5.

PETER, ISABEL, SANDRA, DIRK.

DIRK:

I turned on the TV and I knew everybody – they were all people I knew or friends or friends of friends. She was my girlfriend, before she was on telly every night, in the days when nobody knew her, and he and I used to go out drinking all night.

It's like a ghost train.

Then: commercial break. And I know the guy in the ad too. There's a man carrying a woman across a big puddle. Frankie.

And I change channel: more ads, what a coincidence, the same ad, Frankie. And I change channel again: there are ads everywhere and always the same ad, Frankie, on three channels simultaneously.

Brief pause.

ISABEL:

A piece of bread. A fried egg.

A pepper mill.

Brief pause.

SANDRA:

That's what he won this prize for and he says he despises the jury and doesn't need the money any more.

Brief pause.

But he'll have it anyway.

Brief pause.

Sure. I'd have done the same.

ISABEL:

I was going to do a show about Paradise Lost but no-one here was interested. Heaven and Hell: you can do something with that.

The battle of the angels. Better than a bunch of cleaners.

5.2

PETER, SANDRA, ISABEL and DIRK begin to take off their animal masks and costumes. They remove their make-up. They handle the individual pieces with great care; the fur, hair, wigs, horns, beaks, manes, hooves, claws.

Then they all have showers. As this is going on:

PETER:

Maybe we need to retrain. I've seen these girls on MTV, singing and dancing, all these girls, loads of girls, shaking their bodies. Who teaches them that. There are people who do that sort of thing, who teach girls that sort of thing. Who are they? How do you get to do that?

ISABEL:

You've given your baby away?

Brief pause.

Because if you didn't you wouldn't have time for this –

Brief pause.

Is it true, you've given your baby away? Is that true?

PETER:

You're going to do *what*?

Pause.

DIRK:

Yeah, I thought –

Pause.

PETER:

You're not going to –

DIRK:

Yeah, I am – at the gala –

PETER:

You do not want to do that! That –

DIRK:

I –

PETER:

That –

DIRK:

It's – at the gala benefit

PETER:

You don't want that, you do not really want –

You want –

Pause. They start to dry themselves off.

You want –

Brief pause.

To call Frankie?

Pause.

DIRK:
Yeah –

PETER:
Call him –

DIRK:
Call him – yeah, at the –

PETER:
Why?

DIRK:
Frankie's alright.

PETER:
What?

DIRK:
No –

PETER:
What?

DIRK:
What's, I mean, what's wrong with Frankie – at the gala –

PETER:
At the gala –

DIRK:
I went to this gala benefit –

ISABEL:

> 500 Euros a plate.

DIRK:

> And I met someone who might finance the cleaners, the story of the men dressed up as cleaning women –

> *Brief pause.*

> He's interested in it –

> *Brief pause.* PETER *turns round very slowly to face* DIRK.

> He's interested in it, he thinks it's good, I told him the story –

> *Pause.*

PETER:

> Yeah?

> *Brief pause.*

DIRK:

> Yeah!

> *Brief pause.*

> But they want a name. Or a face.

> *Pause.*

> Someone like Frankie.

> *Pause.*

PETER:

> Frankie spent six years being the zebra and now he's carrying a woman across a puddle on television. In a twenty second ad.

DIRK:

> Doesn't matter – he reckons it's the face that counts.

PETER:

> Frankie can't do anything.

DIRK:

He reckons, it needs a rainmaker. Someone that people in other countries have already seen – he said, nothing's going to happen without Frankie.

Brief pause.

Nothing's going to happen without Frankie.

As soon as they have finished showering and getting dried, the four start putting on new costumes. PETER gets into his FRIED EGG costume, DIRK becomes a BOTTLE OF KETCHUP, the squeezy kind, ISABEL has a PEPPER MILL costume which, like the others, is not easy to get on. SANDRA's costume is the PIECE OF TOAST. Unlike the animal costumes, these costumes are much less expressive, more unambiguous.

6.

Darkness. Music. PETER, DIRK, SANDRA and ISABEL as THE FRIED EGG, THE PIECE OF TOAST, THE PEPPER MILL and THE KETCHUP BOTTLE.

THE FRIED EGG, THE PIECE OF TOAST, THE PEPPER MILL
AND THE BOTTLE OF KETCHUP:

Darkness. Music. The lights come up slowly. At the front of the stage, standing in a row facing the audience: a fried egg, a piece of toast, a pepper mill, a bottle of ketchup. Waiting, earnest, uncertain.
For a long time nothing happens. Occasionally the four exchange looks – as far as their costumes permit.

An imperceptible movement. Are the fried egg and the piece of toast shuffling closer together?
It's possible.
Yes they are, they are shuffling closer together, they're getting closer.

The pepper mill can turn her head. It makes a grinding sound.
The squeezy ketchup bottle can lift up its top and close it again, later the top will weaken and pop open by itself.

The yolk in the middle of the fried egg is soft but not so soft that it breaks straight away.

They dance a little bit on the spot, as far as they can. Now and again they mount each other.

Pepper mill and ketchup bottle snog each other.

The fried egg and piece of toast rub against each other. The egg breaks slightly. The toast too slowly comes apart.

Until this point the four objects have made no sound but now the toast can't help sighing with pain.

The pepper mill has found a way to torture the ketchup bottle. Now the ketchup bottle starts to leak red fluid.

The toast and fried egg are in a dreadful state and separate.

Someone uses an aluminium fish slice as a telephone.

The piece of toast goes up to the pepper. What a relief. They hug.

The egg leans against the injured ketchup bottle: but what's going to come of this?

The pepper mill jumps around on top of the piece of toast.

The fried egg gives up, maybe starts to eat itself.

The ketchup bottle mistreats the pepper mill and in the process leaks more and more thick, red fluid.

The lights slowly fade into darkness.

The end.

The End.

IDOMENEUS

Idomeneus was given its world premiere at the Cuvilliéstheater Munich on 15th June 2008 with the following cast:

Ulrike Arnold, Sibylle Canonica, Anna Riedl, Anne Schäfer, Eva Schuckardt, Heide von Strombeck, Lisa Wagner, Ulrich Beseler, Stefan Hunstein, Shenja Lacher, Felix Rech, Arnulf Schumacher, Helmut Stange, Stefan Wilkening.

It was directed by Dieter Dorn.

This translation was first performed on 18th August 2012 at the DCASE Storefront Theatre 66 East Randolph St, Chicago with the following cast:

McKenzie Chinn, Katy Carolina Collins, Joshua Davis, Joey deBettencourt, Matt Fletcher, Hank Hilbert, Ann James, Susaan Jamshidi, Danny Junod, Lona Livingston, Karie Miller, Kyra Morris, Cody Proctor, Dylan Stuckey, Nate Whelden.

It was directed by Jonathan L. Green for Sideshow Theatre Company.

It was premiered in the UK at the Gate Theatre on 19th June 2014 with the following cast:

Alex Austin, Jon Foster, Mark Monero, Susie Trayling, Ony Uhiara

It was directed by Ellen McDougall for The Gate Theatre.

A group of between ten and fourteen men and women.
Possibly more.

A very cautious pace to start with.

Clear breaks between scenes.

1

A MAN AND A WOMAN,
BOTH NO LONGER YOUNG:
Idomeneus,
King of Crete,

returning home
from Troy,

the city that had fallen
after ten years of war

with his eighty ships
the eighty ships

he'd set out with
ten years before
for Troy
to crush the city and its inhabitants,

FOUR WOMEN, FOUR GENERATIONS:
and with all the men
on those eighty ships
who were still alive
after ten years of war

A DIFFERENT WOMAN AND A DIFFERENT MAN:
Idomeneus
the Cretan King

returning home from Troy
coming home to Crete

is caught

FOUR WOMEN, FOUR MEN:
> in a storm,
> in a hurricane,
>
> so terrible
> that none of the ships
> not one of them
> none of the eighty

A MAN OF FIFTY:
> except the ship belonging to the King himself,
> can withstand the towering waves,
>
> just one ship,

ALL:
> only one out of eighty,

TWO:
> the King's ship,

ALL:
> the others,
> all of them,
>
> all the other ships
> sink in the storm,
>
> and the men on those ships
> drown in the mountainous waves,

A FEW, SPREAD OUT:
> the great ships
> fill with water the moment they capsize
>
> and then:

ONE:

    they hurtle straight down into the deep

    dragging a thick veil
    of bubbles behind them,

TWO:

    and with those ships,

A GROUP:

    trapped inside them,

A WOMAN:

    the men sink to the bottom
    of the sea

THREE WOMEN:

    the men, the soldiers, the warriors
    but not only them:

    the women as well,
    the hostages, prisoners,

    the slaves,
    and children too.

THREE OTHER WOMEN:

    All of them struggling, fighting
    desperately

    hopelessly
    helplessly

    for their lives, their bare lives,
    and dying anyway,

FIVE DIFFERENT PEOPLE:

    drowning, perishing –

regardless
young and old. It takes them all.

A MAN:

The King,
no longer young after ten years of war,
Idomeneus,
who has seen many people go to their deaths, a great many,
shouts at the sea,
at God,

TWO WOMEN, ONE MAN:

the storm,
the waves,

these are the last moments
of his life,
he knows.

SIX PEOPLE WHO DON'T UNDERSTAND:

Why is he shouting,
why can't he make peace

with his fate,
why is there no acceptance,
only anger and wrath?

TWO WOMEN:

This end,
God,

after everything that's happened?

A MAN:

After everything that's happened,

is this the end?

THREE PEOPLE WHO HAVE TO GET ON WITH EACH OTHER:
After everything
that's happened,

after the war,
after waiting in the Trojan horse,

after surviving
and the vast slaughter

how should
how could

the ending make sense?

This ending,
not in the war,

but on the way home,
at sea.

A WOMAN:
The fear,
the fear of dying,

has not changed in those years,

ANOTHER WOMAN:
yes it has:

it has grown, it is greater now
than it ever was,

BOTH:
during the war

the fear
of death

grew with every day,

before,
when they set out for Troy,

they had little more
than an inkling of death,

but now,
now Idomeneus has seen enough,

he knows
where that journey leads:

horror,
and pain.

A MAN, A WOMAN, BOTH NO LONGER YOUNG:
You have nothing to fear,
you have nothing to fear,
you only have to journey down
to the bottom of the sea
into the cold.

SEVEN PEOPLE:
Mute with fear,
Idomeneus,

THE WOMAN FROM THE BEGINNING:
the Cretan King,

SEVEN PEOPLE:
thinks he hears a voice
in the roaring of the hurricane

a question:

THREE PEOPLE:
> What
> what would you promise
> to stay alive?
> If you survive
>
> all this,
> what will you do then?

THE MAN FROM THE BEGINNING:
> I
> I will,
>
> if we are spared from drowning,
> my men and I,

ANOTHER MAN, POSSIBLY RATHER HOARSE:
> if our ship is preserved intact,
> if we reach the shore of Crete alive,
>
> I will sacrifice the first living thing we meet,
>
> whatever it may be,
> whoever it may be.

FIVE DISAPPOINTED PEOPLE:
> A sacrifice –
> what an offer.

THREE PEOPLE WHO WANTED TO DO EVERYTHING DIFFERENTLY:
> It's more like a lottery –
> sacrifice one life –
> and for that
> you keep your own,
> a swap.

THE TWO LEFT ALONE:

What a suggestion,
whatever it may be,
whoever it may be.

THREE OTHERS:

Wouldn't it be better
if Idomeneus followed the men
on his seventy-nine lost ships down to the underworld?

THE TWO:

He shouts and shouts:
What have I lived and fought for

if I must die like this.
My time has not yet come!

A NO LONGER VERY YOUNG WOMAN WITH A BAG:

God has prepared a death
for all of us.

THE YOUNG ONES:

The wind dies down,
slowly.
The storm fades,
gradually.

The waters grow calm.
The clouds part.

Wreckage.
What's left of the lost ships.

The sun.
Idomeneus is alive.

THE OLD ONES:
>But now,
>as the crests of the waves ripple gently,
>
>the Cretan King is overcome by a fear
>which is worse
>
>than the fear of dying ever was,
>a fear, totally unexpected,
>
>a burden on him
>heavy as lead,
>
>one which lames him,
>guilt, a sense of what's to come,
>
>almost enough to make him blind,
>blind,
>
>so at first he doesn't see
>what lies before him:
>
>the island of Crete in the morning sun.

ONE OF THEM:
>Home, Crete.

ANOTHER:
>Let us turn around, men,
>and find our end on the open sea.

THE THIRD:
>We cannot be here,
>fate had foreseen a different ending for us.

ALL THREE:
>That is what Idomeneus,
>King of the island before them in the sun,

who has returned home from Troy,
the city that had fallen after ten years of war,

who has now reached his destination, his native shore,
that is what he wants to say to his crew,

but he does not say it.

A WOMAN:
He thinks:

TWO WOMEN:
This shore harbours something worse
than anything we have ever encountered.

A WOMAN OF SEVENTY:
Worse
than anything we have ever encountered.

Yet he also hopes nevertheless:

A WOMAN OF SEVENTY AND A YOUNG WOMAN:
Everything will be alright.

2.

SIX WOMEN AND MEN:

Olive trees.

FOUR OTHERS:

Grass and scrubland scorched by the sun.
Stones.

TWO OTHERS:

A decaying labyrinth.

SEVEN:

its walls
covered in lichen.

A WOMAN:

The wind.

A YOUNG MAN:

Up
on the hill,
in the city,

at a window
in the royal palace
the head of a young man

A WOMAN:

that's Idomeneus's son
Idamantes
he's about eighteen or twenty

TWO YOUNG MEN:
> Idamantes,
> who was a child
> when his father went to war

> he stares at the sea, searching.

> He said
> he'd come back.
> A promise is a promise.

A GROUP OF MEN:
> That stare into the distance,
> out across the sea.
> What a storm that was last night,
> what a storm.
> When will his father's ships come home?

A GROUP OF WOMEN:
> Where are they?
> Which of them are still alive?

A YOUNG MAN:
> What's that shadow on the sea?

> Is that a ship?
> It's big, but there are no sails –
> maybe it's a wreck with not a soul left on board?

3.

THREE WOMEN:
> Elsewhere,
> in another room in the palace,
> a woman who's still young,
> an old man.
>
> He's doing it with her.
> She's doing it with him.
> They're doing it together.

THREE MEN:
> They're panting.

A WOMAN:
> Early morning.

THREE WOMEN:
> What is he doing to her?

THREE WOMEN, THREE MEN:
> They groan
> let everyone hear it
> let everyone hear it
>
> slip slap
> slip slap

THREE MEN:
> She's Meda,
> Queen of Crete,
> wife of Idomeneus,
> still a young woman,
> alone for ten years,

A WOMAN:

>He's Nauplius,
>King of Nauplia,
>a slave trader,
>once one of Jason's crew,
>an Argonaut,

THREE MEN:

>now an old man

>and a fucker.

THREE WOMEN, THREE MEN:

>They groan,
>let everyone hear it,
>let everyone hear it,

>slip slap
>slip slap

A WOMAN, NO LONGER YOUNG:

>what is he doing to that young woman –

4.

A MAN:

On the shore,

ANOTHER MAN:

on the shore,

A WOMAN:

nothing.

THE FIRST MAN:

Cliffs, sand, stones,

waves. Apart from that, nothing. A couple of trees.

THE WOMAN:

No lizards. No stray dogs, no beetles.

Not even a bird in the sky.

Nothing at all, nobody there.

THE SECOND MAN:

The King's eyes dart back and forth.
The beach is empty, deserted, no beast,
no man –

is that a sign?

THE FIRST MAN:

It is a sign.

ALL THREE:

Of what though?

THE WOMAN:

> The King's eyes dart back and forth.

THE WOMAN AND ONE MAN:

> No music. No drums and trumpets.
> Where is the
> welcoming committee?
> The King is back! Idomeneus!

THE FIRST MAN:

> There,
> in the distance,
> something's moving.
>
> Something slowly approaches
> zigzagging
> jumping over the rocks,
> what is it?
> Is it an animal?
>
> Zig zag
> that's not an animal,
> that's a man,
>
> he's jumping, leaping even, dancing,
> he's waving,
> he's excited,
> he's happy,

THE FIRST MAN AND THE WOMAN:

> zig zag,
> he's shouting,
>
> it's a young man,
> he's shouting: Hello, hello?

THE WOMAN:
Who are you?

Up there, in the city
I saw your ship,
a shadow on the water,

I am
Idamantes,
son of Idomeneus

THE WOMAN AND THE SECOND MAN:
once King of Crete,
absent for ten years,

and who are you,
asks the young man and looks
into the burnt, scarred faces of the seafarers,
have you come from Troy?

THE SECOND MAN AND THE WOMAN:
What can you tell
of Idomeneus,
my father,
once King of Crete,
and of the eighty ships,
he took to war?

Did you
see them sink?

Silence.

And what have you pledged to do
if one day you
should set foot on home soil?

THE WOMAN:

> What have you sacrificed
> to reach home alive?

> What was the price?

THE FIRST MAN:

> Then the King draws his knife
> and cuts the boy's throat.

> Butchers him, bleeds him dry,
> a wave of blood spurts out from his quivering body,

> to the horror of the men
> in a circle
> around the lost boy.

THE WOMAN:

> And when the blood reaches their feet
> the men seize the King of Crete,

THE FIRST MAN:

> Idomeneus,

THE SECOND MAN:

> and hang him naked
> head down
> from a tree

THE FIRST MAN:

> they skin him alive

THE WOMAN:

> and they cut him open,
> drag his guts out onto the beach
> and make a chain out of them
> for the King.

THE FIRST MAN:

What have I lived and fought for
if I must die like this.
My time has not yet come!

THE SECOND MAN:

It wasn't like that:

THE WOMAN:

that's not what happened.

THE FIRST MAN:

This is what happened:

My son

says the father to the quivering boy,

THE WOMAN:

don't you recognize your old father?
Come here, let me hold you in my arms,
my darling child, come, come –

he hugs his son,

THE SECOND MAN:

my father, my dear father,

THE WOMAN:

and turns his gaze back
onto the calm sea.

What's going to come from there?
Will something come?

THE FIRST MAN:

What is going to come from there?
The waves roll slowly onto the beach:

a promise is a promise.
A promise is a promise.

THE WOMAN:

Not his son –
who would sacrifice his son?

THE FIRST MAN:

What God
can demand that –
not his son.

The circle of men returned home,
grey now, old.

THE WOMAN:

The empty beach.

THE SECOND MAN:

The young man. Idamantes. The son.

THE FIRST MAN:

What a gift.

THE THREE:

The waves.

A promise is a promise.
A promise is a promise.

5.

    Nauplius:
    old,
    out of shape,

TWO OTHER MEN:

    does with Meda,
    wife of Idomeneus, not yet forty,
    or demands of her
    things

    that she's never done before,
    that she'd never have allowed before,

ANOTHER MAN:

    but now
    after waiting ten years –

TWO MEN:

    Nauplius: King of Nauplia
    and slave trader,

    and in his young days,
    before he got fat,

ANOTHER MAN:

    an Argonaut,

THE FOUR MEN:

    a man who'd sweated blood.
    Companion of Heracles and Orpheus.

    Had a son and lost him.

TWO WOMEN:

And that's what Nauplius seeks to avenge.

FOUR MEN:

The slave trader's son
was a man of letters.
One who could even
invent letters.
Palamedes.

ONE OF THE WOMEN:

Look, Dad,
I've invented a letter:

ONE OF THE WOMEN AND THE OTHER WOMAN:

Like this and this and this.
Drawing in the air. An A. A for alpha.

A WOMAN:

A, a beginning,
everyone says A all the time, but no-one can write it,
we need an alphabet,
Palamedes' Dad.
I've found a beginning for the alphabet!

A MAN:

My boy: and what end will you find?

The end was like this:
Palamedes was cleverer than Odysseus.

THREE MEN:

The cunning Odysseus pretended to be mad
when the Greeks sailed for Troy, however,
Palamedes exposed Odysseus's cowardice, for which
Odysseus hated him.
He set a trap for Palamedes,

and he had Palamedes,
the brainy one,
discoverer of the letter A,
stoned to death
in front of his own people
in the camp outside Troy.

A MAN:

The old Argonaut,
Nauplius, father of Palamedes,
set off himself
on the long journey from Nauplia
to the Greek camp outside Troy,
to fetch his dead son,
and to kill the cunning Odysseus in single combat.

But the Generals of the Greek armies,

THE TWO WOMEN:

Men like Menelaus and Agamemnon
and Idomeneus, King of Crete,
leader of a mighty fleet
of eighty ships,
a powerful man,

would not let Odysseus go,
he was their best man,
they needed him,
they forbade single combat
because they knew:

Nauplius, the Argonaut,
had once, together with his comrades,
carried the Argo across the Sahara desert,

he would have flattened Odysseus.

FOUR MEN:

No single combat.

A WOMAN:

So Nauplius travelled home with his son's body,

TWO WOMEN:

and this was his revenge against the Greek Generals,
who had denied him
his right
to fight Odysseus:

TWO MEN:

he fucked their wives,
all of them,
one by one,

TWO OTHER MEN:

got some of them pregnant,

A WOMAN:

and if he couldn't fuck
or impregnate them himself,

TWO WOMEN:

because he wasn't a young man any more
and couldn't be everywhere
at the same time

then he at least gave them the idea,

A WOMAN:

Look, Clytemnestra,
this is Aigisthus – what do you think of him?

TWO WOMEN:

What do you think of him?

THE FOUR MEN:

   She got thinking.

THE TWO WOMEN:

   And the Generals
   in Troy
   hear about it, but they can't leave,

A MAN:

   Dear Odysseus,
   that little freckle
   on the inside
   of her right thigh –
   mmmmm.
   Yours Nauplius.

THE TWO WOMEN:

   And when Odysseus
   came home to Ithaca
   after ten years of war
   and ten years of wandering
   his son Telemachus
   had a little eleven year old brother
   with red hair.

THE FOUR MEN:

   And when Idomeneus
   came home to Crete
   after ten years of war
   Nauplius was there waiting for him
   in Idomeneus's bed.

6.

SIX MEN AND WOMEN:

Olive trees.
Grass and scrubland scorched by the sun.
Stones.

FOUR OTHERS:

A decaying labyrinth,
its walls
covered in lichen.

SOME OF THE WOMEN:

The wind.

SEVEN MEN AND WOMEN:

Up
on the hill,
in the city:

Idomeneus,
the King,
hand in hand with his son Idamantes,
back from the war.
He and the few survivors.

A MAN AND A WOMAN:

Is only one ship coming back?
Were are the others?
Where are the other men?

A WOMAN:

And there stands
Meda
the Queen, still young.

ANOTHER WOMAN:

> He can see it in her eyes, instantly:
> she has been faithful to him,
> she has waited, ten years,
> there's no Nauplius here,

A MAN:

> and there never was any Nauplius, not here.

ANOTHER MAN:

> The whole thing,

A THIRD MAN:

> Everything about Nauplius

TWO WOMEN:

> A rumour, an invention,

A MAN:

> Rubbish.

TWO MEN:

> It's rubbish.

A MAN:

> Isn't it?

TWO MEN:

> Ten years –

A MAN, NO LONGER YOUNG:

> My wife –

A WOMAN, NOT YET FORTY:

> My husband –

BOTH:

> To see you again.

THE WOMAN:

Thank God.

THE MAN:

Yes.

A YOUNG WOMAN:

How should they spend the day?

THREE BEST FRIENDS (FEMALE):

How? Where do they begin? How can they pick up from
where they left off?
What do they say?
If they were alone –

A WOMAN:

Were there women in Troy?
There must have been women there.

A MAN:

That's not how the conversation starts.

ANOTHER MAN:

And what women is she talking about?
The ones in the camp?

Or the ones in Troy,
when they ransacked the city?

THE MAN FROM BEFORE:

That's not how the conversation starts.

THE WOMAN:

You swore
to sacrifice your son?
Our son?

THE MAN:

Not our son.
The first living thing
I met on the shore –

and that was our son.

THE WOMAN:

Our child – and now?
Yes, kill it: that's the price.

THE MAN:

The price of what?

THE WOMAN:

The price of survival. The price of survival
is the death of our children,
fuck me,
I can give you new children,
kill the boy.

How many parents
see their children die?

How many carry their children's corpses out of the rubble
of their destroyed homes?
And live on. Or die later.
Why should we be different?
Didn't you yourself
kill children
in Troy? Go on then.
Just because it's your own child,
this time, is no reason to wait,
it's just the same.

THE MAN FROM BEFORE:

That's not how the conversation starts.

7.

A MAN:

>The first night.
>The first night
>home.
>
>Idomeneus,
>King of Crete,
>
>enters the bedroom
>from the left
>
>and she,
>Meda,
>
>after a while,
>from the right.

THE MAN AND A WOMAN:

>Silence. Uncertainty.

THE MAN:

>After everything
>that's happened.

THE WOMAN:

>Don't we need
>to talk?

THE MAN:

>What is there to talk about,
>let's –

TWO MEN, ONE WOMAN:

>There it is:

suspicion.
Doubt.
Mistrust.

Hesitation.

A MAN:

And that's how Nauplius
who perhaps never
set foot on Crete

A WOMAN:

who perhaps never
touched the King's wife,

A MAN:

is in the room anyway.
Lying in the bed.

Stretching out and burping
and stinking.

SEVEN:

The King,
Idomeneus,

sees his beautiful wife
Meda

after ten years of war
after ten years' absence,

he looks at her,
the naked King,

who now knows with increasing certainty:
she was unfaithful,

she was unfaithful to him
the whole time.

A WOMAN:

But nothing happened.

SEVEN:

Force,

A WOMAN:

she defends herself.

ONE MAN:

no-one comes.

A WOMAN:

Better
if something had happened.

TWO MEN:

So:
Nauplius, King of Nauplia,
slave trader,
seducer,
former Argonaut,
companion of Heracles and of Orpheus,
whom ten years before Idomeneus had refused the right,
to defend the honour
of his son Palamedes stoned to death by Odysseus,

silently entered
the room, unnoticed.

A MAN AND A WOMAN:

He strikes.

ANOTHER MAN:

> A,
> did you know
> my son, Palamedes,
> invented
> the letter A,
> the first letter of the alphabet?

A MAN:

> Come,
> said Nauplius,
> let us spell
> the beginning of our alphabet,
> and the end, that my son Palamedes
> found through Odysseus:
> A and O.

THREE WOMEN:

> But
> Idomeneus is still alive.
>
> Nauplius, the Argonaut,
> strikes again and again,
> laboriously, tortuously,
>
> yet Idomeneus
> dies and does not die.
> He cannot die.

TWO MEN:

> Killing
> does not work.

ANOTHER MAN:

> Maybe something like a bargain
> protects Idomeneus,

TWO WOMEN:

or an unfulfilled promise.

FOUR MEN:

For that Nauplius makes himself
the new King of Crete,

A WOMAN:

marries
or kills
the wife,
kills the son,
and exiles the old king,
has him
exiled, taken away
by a fisherman,

A MAN:

has him exiled to another shore,
far away from Crete.

8.

A MAN:

> The first night.
> The first night home.

A WOMAN:

> Idomeneus,
> King of Crete,

THE MAN:

> enters the bedroom
> from the left
>
> and she

THE WOMAN:

> Meda,
>
> after a while
> from the right.
>
> Silence. Uncertainty.

THE MAN:

> After everything
> that's happened.

THE WOMAN AND THE MAN:

> Meda and Idomeneus,
>
> reunited after ten years.
>
> They kiss,
> they make love.

They talk.
They travel through those ten lost years.

THE MAN:

Tell me
how our child grew up.

THE WOMAN:

Talk about Troy. About the war.

THE WOMAN AND THE MAN:

The war.
The child.

The war.
The child.

The war:

THE MAN:

how I –

THE WOMAN:

The child: when he was fifteen years old

and wanted to get married,

THE MAN:

at fifteen?

BOTH:

Quiet laughter.

THE MAN:

Marry? Who?

THE WOMAN:

A girl.

THE MAN:

What kind of girl?

THE WOMAN:

A fisherman's daughter.

THE MAN:

Oh no.

BOTH:

Laughter, quiet laughter, laughter.

THE MAN:

A fisherman's daughter.

And?

THE WOMAN:

She got pregnant.

THE MAN:

No! By him? Good, good!

THE WOMAN:

And Troy?

THE MAN:

Where is the child?

THE WOMAN:

Gone.

THE MAN:

Where?

THE WOMAN:

With the girl.

THE MAN:

Is the child a boy or a girl?

THE WOMAN:

No idea. I never asked.

THE MAN:

Why not? And her, the young mother?

THE WOMAN:

Lives with her father, the fisherman.

THE MAN:

And the boy, Idamantes?

THE WOMAN:

Fell in love with another girl soon afterwards
and now loves a different girl again.

THE MAN:

Who?

THE WOMAN:

Electra.

THE MAN:

Electra?

THE WOMAN:

Agamemnon's daughter.

THE MAN AND THE WOMAN:

A soft whistle through his teeth,
a soft whistle of recognition through his teeth.

Why? Why Electra? Is she here?

THE WOMAN:

    That's right: she's here.

THE MAN:

    Why?

THE WOMAN:

    I don't know. Nobody at home wants her.

9.

THREE MEN:

> And this fisherman,
> the father of the girl
>
> that Idamantes, the son of Idomeneus,
> got pregnant
>
> aged fifteen,
> that same fisherman
>
> will later prove
> the King of Crete's
>
> downfall:
> he can't be killed –
>
> let him starve somewhere.

THREE WOMAN:

> In the boat the fisherman and the King.
>
> A glorious day, calm seas.

THREE MEN:

> The fisherman:
> Your son
> was a randy bastard.
>
> Your son
> fucked my child.
>
> Your son,
> how he stank,
> after two days

in the fields,
rotting,
next to Mama Mama,
she would have found that funny,
she would have said:
I love grandchildren.
I love grandchildren.

10

THE MAN AND THE WOMAN:
>Giggling giggling, laughing softly
>happily reunited,
>Meda and Idomeneus,
>the happy couple,

>how could we
>lose ten years,

>let's pretend
>we never lost them,

>laughing at their son's first love
>slightly coarse, slightly drunk:
>the cunt, the little cunt.

>Then they sleep.

11.

A WOMAN, NO LONGER YOUNG:
> The sea
> in the moonlight.

A GROUP OF WOMEN:
> Out of the eighty ships
> seventy-nine sank,
>
> seventy-nine,
>
> with them the men, the many men,
> whose wives now, or whose mothers now,
> or whose children now
>
> that the King is back again
> know
>
> that all the others drowned.

TWO WOMEN:
> That makes
> four thousand women,
>
> widows and mothers,

ONE WOMAN:
> or more.

BOTH:
> They search the beach at night.
> Each one alone. They wander around.

A GROUP OF WOMEN:

    They wander around the beach at night,
    lots of them, thousands.

THE FIRST WOMAN:

    The sea in the moonlight.
    The tide brings in a few remnants of the ships.

    The sea is generous tonight.
    The tide brings in the bodies of the drowned.
    Not all, but some.

TWO WOMEN:

    Is that, that's the husband of –
    here,
    here, this is,
    one woman shouts,
    at least it could be him,
    and that,

ANOTHER WOMAN:

    that could be,
    that's –

BOTH WOMEN:

    This one could be
    at least it could be him,
    here,
    this is –

THE FIRST WOMAN:

    Shouts on the beach at night.

12.

A MAN AND A WOMAN AND A YOUNG MAN:

The next morning
all is well.

Who can say that:
all is well.

Breakfast,
father, mother,
son,

THE MAN AND THE YOUNG MAN:

and you
and you really,

the father asks, proud
and you and this girl really

you got her,
no, no, I really don't
want to hurt your feelings,

I thought you
if you want we can bring her back, can't we?
Are you sure you don't? Fine –

THE MAN AND THE WOMAN:

Family. At home at last.

THE MAN:

Sometimes the King thinks:

if someone were to come through the door now and hack
everything to pieces

(like in Troy)
destroy everything.

There wasn't such a big difference between us and them,
none of it should have ever happened,

there aren't such big differences between people,
that they can't live with each other

or without each other.

THE YOUNG MAN:

The son says something:

THE MAN:

What? What was that, what did you say, my son,
I was thinking,

BOTH:

what did you want to say to me, please say it again.

THE YOUNG MAN:

The son: I love a girl.

THE MAN:

The father: wonderful. What's the name of this girl?

THE YOUNG MAN:

The son: Electra.

THE MAN:

The father: Electra – the daughter of Agamemnon and
Clytemnestra.

Good, good. Just one question:
why is she here?

BOTH:
　　Why isn't she in Mycenae
　　with her mother waiting for her father,

　　who will surely return home
　　soon just like me,

　　or has maybe even
　　arrived home already?

　　You will have to ask her father,
　　my son,
　　if he'll give you his daughter.

　　If someone were to come through the door now and hack
　　everything to pieces –

THE WOMAN:
　　A man enters the room.
　　Pale, white, as if in shock, not saluting.

A PALE MAN:
　　A disaster has befallen the island of Crete.
　　In the very east of the island
　　a whale was washed up ashore,

　　and when the men
　　cut the whale open

　　inside the whale they found a living cow,
　　which was pregnant,
　　and gave birth to a wolf.

THE WOMAN, THE MAN AND THE YOUNG MAN:
　　A wolf from a cow.

THE PALE MAN:

A wolf with calves' hooves.
An abomination.

And a horse has given birth to a foal
with the paws of a cat! And now
the wolfcalf is riding the horsecat
and eating it alive.

THE MAN:

Horrible.

THE OTHER MAN:

And the wolfcalf can talk.

THE MAN:

What does it say?

THE OTHER MAN:

It says –

THE MAN:

It says –

THE OTHER MAN:

It says –

THE MAN:

What?

THE OTHER:

It says its name is

Idamantes.

THE MAN:

Idamantes?

THE OTHER:
Idamantes, like your son.
It says it wants its Daddy,
Idomeneus,
King of Crete.

13.

TWO MEN:

On Mount Ida:
Idomeneus and the monster. Facing each other.

TWO WOMEN:

They look at each other.
The monster really is

THE WOMAN AND THE MEN:

a mixture of calf and wolf,
calves' hooves, the teeth of a wolf.

TWO MEN:

Idomeneus,
just back from ten years of war.

He speaks to the chimera:
Where do you come from?

THE TWO WOMEN:

And the beast really does speak:

A MAN AND A WOMAN:

You know that,
you brought me with you.

A MAN:

I brought –

A MAN AND A WOMAN:

Yes, you did, you –

TWO MEN:
     He asks
     the thing its name.

A MAN AND A WOMAN:
     The answer:
     Idamantes,

     you know that,
     I am your child.

     Take me in your arms.
     I am hungry. Give me milk.

     No, give me sea water,
     I like drinking sea water best of all.

     Daddy, daddy.
     Don't pick up that stone.

     don't throw that stone at me,
     don't kill me,

     I'm your child.
     Take me with you.

     You should kill
     the other thing,

     the young man,
     who's taken my place in your house,

     who wants to take away
     my bride,

     I already spoke to her father,
     Agamemnon, ages ago:

I met him on the way to hell,
chopped up with an axe,

and Agamemnon told me,
Electra must kill her mother first,
and then I can marry her.

A MAN:

We have reached
the boundary
between reason
and superstition.

Can anyone
reasonably explain
the violent death of a human being?
No.

The sacrifice of a human life
or many human lives,
is nothing
but an unholy alliance of conformism and fear,
greed and guilt,

believing in this
the cause that demands it,
the right to do it,
its apparent necessity

nothing, a delusion,
which nevertheless

can easily destroy someone,
only too easily,

TWO MEN, TWO WOMEN:

and it is uncertain

whether we ever cross
the boundary between reason
and superstition.

You,
the King says to the monster,
can't do anything to me,
you're not there,
I'm stronger,
a thousand times stronger than you.

A MAN AND A WOMAN:

But who can talk like that,
who has the right

to talk like that
after he's burnt down a city?

Who can talk like that
after he's sent thousands
to their deaths?

The human sacrifice has already happened,
it is happening,
all the time:

others are dead,
others are dying,
and you're alive.

The monster laughs:
human flesh,

who knows the smell
of dead flesh better than you?

TWO WOMEN, TWO MEN:
   The monster
   transforms itself
   into a bee and into a shark
   and flies away.

14.

A WOMAN:

> Electra is the daughter of Agamemnon
> and Clytemnestra,
>
> the sister of Iphigenia,
> the sister of Chrysothemis and Orestes.
>
> Agamemnon sacrificed Iphigenia,
> and for that Clytemnestra will kill him,
>
> or she already has done,
> and for that,
>
> Clytemnestra killing Agamemnon,
> Electra and her brother Orestes will
>
> kill their mother, Clytemnestra,
> and her lover Aigisthus.
>
> The daughter should kill her mother.

A MAN:

> Idamantes is the son of Idomeneus and Meda.
> In fear of death Idomeneus pledged a sacrifice,
> to escape a deadly storm,
> and now the father should kill his son.

BOTH:

> Fear. Obligations, rules, laws.
> Honour and respect.
> Revenge and punishment.

THE WOMAN:

> There are reasons for everything.

THE MAN:

What a time
for the mother, the father,

THE MAN AND THE WOMAN:

the children.

THE WOMAN:

The children
want to be happy together.

That was their plan.

THE MAN:

They loved each other,
desired each other wildly,

THE MAN AND THE WOMAN:

they made love gently and playfully,
and they wanted each other
three or four times a day,

THE WOMAN:

or they couldn't touch each other,
strictly forbidden,

BOTH:

but suddenly they are caught in the same net.
Injuries, fear.
Obligations, rules, laws.

THE WOMAN:

Honour and respect
and revenge and punishment.

THE WOMAN:

    And she should
    kill her mother
    and he should let himself be killed by his father,

    and the son says:

THE MAN:

    Dear father,
    before you kill me,
    I will kill you,

    and the daughter says:

THE WOMAN:

    wicked mother,
    before I kill you
    I will kill myself.

THE WOMAN AND THE MAN:

    The lovers
    are caught up in something
    stronger than them
    that they have nothing to do with,

    and that is why
    they go to the harbour at night

THE WOMAN:

    and there they steal
    a little boat,

THE MAN:

    the red Rosie

BOTH:

    and they disappear

    together
    in the Aegean

THE WOMAN:

    the Aegean,
    masterpiece of creation,
    most beautiful of all seas,
    with a million glittering reflections
    of the moon and the sun,

THE MAN AND THE WOMAN:

    and no-one
    has ever
    heard from the young,
    blissfully happy
    and carefree couple
    Electra and Idamantes
    again.

THE WOMAN:

    Only,

    that Electra,
    in anger,

    in terrible anger,

    in an anger
    that spares nothing,

THE MAN:

    never set foot
    on the red boat Rosie
    with Idamantes

and crossed
the Aegean,
masterpiece of creation,
with her lover, her boyfriend,

but on hearing the news
of the cowardly and devious, grotesquely brutal murder
of her father

at the hand of her mother,
set out for Mycenae,

crossing the Aegean,
masterpiece of creation,
blinded to its beauty by her hatred,

and slaughtered her mother,
Clytemnestra,

who ended up lying in a lake of blood,
completely disfigured,

looking into the disfigured face of her own child,
Electra.

THE WOMAN:

This was an act of obligation, rules, law.
Honour and respect.
Revenge, and then came the punishment,
and Electra had to flee and travel

and travel and flee again,
over land and sea,

THE MAN:

she crosses the Aegean
and by day

and during the nights
she thinks about what
she wasn't allowed to experience,
happiness,

THE WOMAN:
rules, laws.

THE MAN:
Honour and respect.
Revenge and punishment.

THE WOMAN:
She thinks
of her mother's disfigured face,
always,

and then she thinks
what her life could have been:

a happy life,
side by side

with young Idamantes,
in his arms:

what a pure pleasure
that was.

ANOTHER MAN (THE SECOND):
And the son says:
Dear father,

before you kill me,
I will kill you,

I will kill you
because I don't want to die,

ANOTHER MAN (THE THIRD):
    and now the question is
    who is stronger,

THE OTHER MAN (THE SECOND):
    and who has more practice,
    experience of killing, of fighting,

THE THIRD MAN:
    it's a question of endurance,

THE SECOND MAN:
    of toughness, of skill, of power, of age,

THE THIRD:
    of cheating,
    of cowardice and bravery,

    of greatness:

    And the son says:

THE FIRST MAN:
    Dear father,

    before you kill me,
    I will kill you,

    if you had sunk
    to the bottom of the sea
    with the seventy-nine other ships

    then the fish and the crabs would have eaten you,
    of course that is not

    a pretty ending,
    but it's better than the other one
    that awaits you now,

and the cold water
in your lungs hurts terribly

but then, so they say,
come the memories

that drive the pain and fear away,
beautiful memories come, images,

while your body slowly sinks down in the deep,
and you open your eyes wide, in the black water,

to see all the beautiful things,
and right at the end,

before the cord of life breaks,
the drowning man remembers
the last time
he swam like this

his lungs full of water:
it was in the warm belly of his mother,
wasn't that wonderful?
Wasn't that wonderful?

You missed that.
Now you've got this.
Before you kill me,
I'm going to kill you.

15.

A GROUP OF WOMEN:

> The Trojan war
> begins with a human sacrifice,
>
> and it ends with a human sacrifice.
> Agamemnon sacrificed his daughter Iphigenia
>
> for wind.
> A lot of wind.

A GROUP OF MEN:

> When Idomeneus,
> King of Crete,
>
> returns
> from the Trojan War
>
> he is caught in a hurricane, wind, a lot of wind,
> and he promises God
>
> a sacrifice,
> to save his own life
> and the lives
> of his crew.

A MAN:

> He kills
> as promised
> the first person
> he meets on his native shore:
>
> it is his own son.

A WOMAN:

The mother of the sacrificed boy
hangs herself.

FIVE PEOPLE WHO UNDERSTAND EACH OTHER ONLY TOO WELL:

As punishment
for this human sacrifice
and the murder of his own child,

the springs on Crete dry up.
The people

are dying of thirst,
but it doesn't take long

for the Cretans
to make the connection
and banish the old King
and thus end an age of superstition.

THREE PEOPLE RIGHT AT THE FRONT:

Freedom.

A RANGE OF FIVE DIFFERENT PEOPLE:

When Idomeneus,
King of Crete,

returns
from the Trojan War

he is caught in a hurricane
and promises God
a sacrifice,

to save his own life
and the lives
of his crew.

147

THREE WOMEN:

But he does not
as promised

kill the first person
he meets on his native shore:

it is his own son.
He kills no-one.

SEVEN MEN:

But he comes home alone,
without the men

who left with him
ten years ago

all of them
do not return.

MANY:

And for the last ten years
the people of Crete have lived very well
without a King.

A MAN:

Soon afterwards
the springs on Crete dry up.

A WOMAN:

The people
are dying of thirst,

but it doesn't take long
for the Cretans

to see a connection
between their thirst

and the return of their King,
and it doesn't take long

for them to banish the King,
Idomeneus,

who says that he
wanted to end an era,

and that's how the people of Crete ended
an era.

16.

THREE MEN:
> A fisherman is to transport him
> to Sicily, in chains.

THE SECOND MAN:
> Do you know
> your son fathered my daughter's child?

THE THIRD MAN:
> A child, yes, a son?

THE FIRST MAN:
> The bright sound of waves cresting on the bow.

THE THREE MEN:
> All could be well,
> everything could be different,
>
> only, it's like this: the end.
> The fisherman, old, bad teeth,
>
> the fisherman,
> father of a deflowered girl,
> and Idomeneus,
> former King of Crete,
> who won the war in Troy and lost everything.

THE SECOND MAN:
> Do you know what you are?
> Do you know what you are?

THE FIRST MAN:
> The fisherman,
> who sometimes,

THE THIRD MAN:

    maybe once or twice an hour,

THE SECOND MAN:

    spits on the banished king.

THE THREE MEN:

    The fisherman brings the banished man
    to the coast of Sicily,

    and having landed,
    breaks all the fingers in his right hand.

    And sets off on the way back, alone.

17.

A GROUP OF WOMEN:

On the beach,
Meda,

who has been waiting for ten years for Idomeneus,
who set off with eighty ships
to destroy Troy,

and Electra,
a young woman, lover of Idamantes,

find
first the butchered boy

bled dry, all white,
with huge eyes, dead and staring,

and then they find
Idomeneus,

King of Crete,
skinned, cut open, gutted,

hanging from a tree,
head down.

18.

A GROUP OF MEN AND WOMEN:
Searing heat.
Idomeneus's gaze follows the boat

make its way towards the horizon.
He raises a hand

to shade his eyes,
to see it, to really see it:

the ship has gone.

A MAN:
The ship has gone.

I'm still alive,
here, look at me,

I've lost everything,
my child, my wife, my home,

my comrades, my ships,
a kingdom,

I am a King -
was a King,

I,
I will

if I escape my downfall,
if I ever reach the shores of Crete again,

I will –

here I am
I'm still alive.

I know what I am,
I know what I am,

I am Idomeneus,
victorious and shipwrecked,
I'm hanging on

to life
I'm hanging on
to life,

and I know
but I know

where the journey leads:

horror,
and pain.

A WOMAN:
On the beach
on the beach

nothing.
Cliffs, sand, stones,

waves. Apart from that, nothing. A few trees.
No lizards. No stray dogs, no beetles.

Not even a bird in the sky.
Nothing at all, nobody there.

The beach is empty, deserted, no beast,
no man –

is that a sign?
It is a sign.

Of what though?
No music. No drums and trumpets.

Where is the
welcoming committee?

There,
in the distance,

something's moving.
Something slowly approaches

zigzagging
jumping over the rocks,

what is it?
Is it an animal?

zig zag
it is an animal,

it's
a dog.

A MAN:

Idomeneus
looks for some twine and finds some
and hangs himself
from a tree naked
head down
that wasn't easy,

he skins himself alive,
and cuts himself open,

drags his guts out onto the beach
and makes himself a chain
out of them.

It wasn't like that:
that's not what happened.
This is what happened:

The waves roll slowly onto the beach:

A promise is a promise.
A promise is a promise.

The empty beach.
The man.

The empty beach.
The man.

Life.
What a gift.
The waves.

A promise is a promise.

I am Idomeneus
and I'm hanging on

to life,
I'm hanging on

to life.

The End.

PEGGY PICKIT SEES THE FACE OF GOD

*My sincere thanks to all those without whose inspiration and
support this work would not have been possible:*

*Ross Manson, Meredith Potter from Volcano, Christina Anderson
and Binyavanga Wainaina, Liesl Tommy, Josette Bushell-Mingo,
Anurita Bains, Weyni Mengesha and Jutta Brendemühl.*

Peggy Pickit was given its world premiere on 15th June 2010 at the Fleck Dance Theatre.

This translation was supported by the Goethe-Institut.

It was first performed on 15th June 2010 at The Fleck Dance Theatre, Toronto with the following cast:

Carol	Maev Beaty
Martin	Trey Lyford
Frank	Tony Nappo
Liz	Jane Spidell

It was directed by Liesl Tommy and commissioned by Ross Manson for Volcano Theatre.

Characters

All four are in their early forties.

FRANK is a consultant in a university hospital, possibly a specialist in infectious diseases.

LIZ worked as a nurse until her daughter was born.

CAROL and MARTIN have spent the last six years working as doctors under very difficult conditions in an improvised clinic somewhere in the developing world.

All four worked together in the same hospital after studying medicine in the same year group.

Setting:

Liz and Frank's house in a university town somewhere in the western world.

FRANK:

It was a total disaster.

An absolute nightmare.

Pause.

What a fucking mess.

Pause.

1.2.

LIZ and FRANK have invited CAROL and MARTIN to their house for dinner.

CAROL and MARTIN have just arrived. The couples greet each other.

LIZ welcomes CAROL, gently.

LIZ:

Hi –

CAROL:

Hi –

LIZ:

Hey!

CAROL:

Hello –

The two women hug warmly for a long time. Old friends. LIZ can't help crying.

FRANK: *(Speechless.)*
Hey, man, hey –

MARTIN: *(Can't stop grinning.)*
Hey, hey –

They hug.

CAROL: *(To the crying LIZ, who still hasn't let go of her.)*
No, no no – don't cry –

LIZ: *(Laughing and crying at the same time.)*
Yes, it's terrible, crying's terrible, I know, I'm terrible,
I'm sorry, I can't help it, I'm so happy –

She wipes her tears away and carries on crying and laughing.

FRANK: *(To MARTIN.)*
Wow! Wow, man, wow!

Short pause.

LIZ:
You're back –

CAROL:
Yes we are – we're back.

FRANK:
You're looking good. You look really good!

1.3.

LIZ:
Even if it wasn't really true. They didn't look bad, they
were tanned, obviously, but they were definitely older.
They'd gone grey, they were older and – worn out.
Knackered. They'd lost a lot of weight, especially him,
Martin.

1.4.

FRANK:
You're looking good. You look really good!

MARTIN:
You too, you look great – how's the family – and where's
– where's –

FRANK: *(Pretending to be shocked, to MARTIN.)*
Your beer gut's gone, where is it, your beer gut – it's gone!
I don't believe it, how did you do that –

MARTIN:

    Where's –

FRANK: *(Suddenly ignores MARTIN and turns to CAROL.)*

    Hey, Carol.

He spreads his arms out. A big gesture.

Welcome. Welcome to Western civilization.
Welcome – home.

CAROL: *(Smiles.)*

    Hi Frank. Thanks. Thank you so much for inviting us.

FRANK hugs CAROL.

MARTIN:

    Liz –

LIZ:

    Martin –

MARTIN and LIZ hug.

LIZ snorts in amusement, not believing this and opens a bottle of champagne, or at least tries to do so. Then she passes the bottle to FRANK.

I mean, just think, the last time we all saw each other we were thirty-five, thirty-five. We were young. And now we're forty-one – forty-one! Six years ago we were young.

Short pause. Blissfully happy.

And now we're old!
Thank God at least we managed to have a child –

She's shocked by her own impertinence.

Uh-oh, Oh my God, no, I shouldn't have said that –

1.5.

CAROL:

    And now we're old. The way she said it –

Short pause.

I didn't get the impression she was talking about her.

Short pause.

I felt she was talking about me.

1.6.

LIZ:

Uh-oh, Oh my God, no, I shouldn't have said that –

CAROL: *(Laughs.)*

Yes, you should, go on, say what you think!
We are old –
(Exaggerating, as if she's describing some apocalyptic decline.)
Soon we'll be all shrivelled up like prunes!

FRANK:

No, wait, wait a minute, you look fantastic – there are no
prunes here.

LIZ: *(Fills their glasses.)*

Quick, let's have a drink, come on, we need a drink,
terrible, I'm terrible –

MARTIN:

No, you're not terrible, you're just being honest –

LIZ:

I am terrible, I mean we've not seen each other for six
years –

FRANK:

Six years!

LIZ:

Whoa – six years. Time goes so fast. Welcome back.

She raises her glass.

FRANK:

Terrible. A nightmare.

Short pause.

She went and slapped her face as hard as she possibly could.

CAROL slaps LIZ in the face.

1.8.

LIZ raises her glass.

Time goes so fast. Welcome back.

MARTIN:

Six years.

CAROL:

A lot's happened. In that time.

LIZ:

A lot.

They drink.

MARTIN:

Six years without champagne.

Short pause.

CAROL:

We brought you something –

1.9.

MARTIN:

I hate dinner parties, I get claustrophobia, always have done. There's only one way to get through a dinner party: alcohol. Without alcohol I couldn't survive.

CAROL:

We brought you something –

LIZ:

What? What is it? You really shouldn't –

CAROL has a paper bag with her.

CAROL:

But of course, well, it's not actually for you, it's for – for –

1.11.1.

FRANK:

She'd forgotten her name. She'd forgotten our daughter's name –

1.11.2.

CAROL:

I'd forgotten her name. I'd forgotten her name, even though I knew her name, I'd been thinking the whole time about what we could bring her, there wasn't much there that you could give a child as a present and then suddenly I couldn't remember her name –

1.12.

CAROL:

We brought you something –

LIZ:

What? What is it? You really shouldn't –

CAROL:

But of course, well, it's not actually for you, it's for – for –

Short pause.

Sorry, I don't believe this –

LIZ:

What's the matter –

CAROL: *(Looks around for help.)*

I don't believe this –

LIZ:

What is it, what's wrong –

CAROL:

I can't remember her name, why can't I remember her
name –

FRANK:

What name –

CAROL: *(Starting to panic.)*

Her name, your daughter's name, I can't believe this –

LIZ:

Kathie –

CAROL:

Kathie! My God! Kathie – of course, whereabouts is she
anyway – where is she?

FRANK:

She's having a sleepover next door. With her friend. Britt.
Awful child.

Short pause.

It's like she's made of plastic.

LIZ:

Stop it –

1.13.

CAROL:

The whole time she wanted to read the letter. She'd laid
the letter out ready so she could read it to us. And she

169

wanted to show us her doll, this plastic figure:
'Peggy Pickit'.

Something like that.

1.14.

FRANK:
Awful child.

Short pause.

It's like she's made of plastic.

LIZ:
Stop it –

CAROL: *(Laughing.)*
Who, who's made of plastic, Britt or Kathie?

FRANK:
Britt, of course. Kathie's great. A living miracle.

Short pause.

Although – maybe I should take a look at her – maybe
Kathie's made of plastic too, who knows, maybe I ought to
examine her more closely –

1.15.

MARTIN:
They had problems, it was obvious. They were really
happy to see us but it was clear that they had problems and
had done for some time.

1.16.1.

CAROL: *(Laughing.)*
Who, who's made of plastic, Britt or Kathie?

FRANK:
Britt, of course, Kathie's great. A living miracle.

Short pause.

Although – maybe I should take a look at her – maybe Kathie's made of plastic too, who knows, maybe I ought to examine her more closely –

CAROL:

Kathie, yeah, – how old is she now –

1.16.2.

LIZ:

Frank never wanted the child.

Short pause.

I did, absolutely. But he didn't. Not really.

Short pause. She bites her lip.

It was that simple.

1.16.3.

CAROL:

Kathie, yeah, – how old is she now –

LIZ: *(Had been caught up in her own thoughts.)*
Kathie? Five. Nearly five and a half.

MARTIN:

Five. Nearly five and a half. And we've never even seen her!

Only on the photos you sent Annie, incredible –

FRANK:

She's huge. A great big lump.

LIZ:

Like you.

LIZ doesn't like FRANK calling the child a 'lump'. Short pause.

Almost as soon as you'd gone, I got pregnant.

MARTIN: *(Trying to be funny.)*
Wait a minute, that means – you two must have had sex, at least once –

FRANK: *(Laughs.)*
Right –

LIZ points to the gift which CAROL and MARTIN have brought with them. The gift is wrapped in plain newspaper or brown paper. You can see that it has traveled a long way.

What is it?

CAROL:
Open it –

LIZ:
But, but you said it's for Kathie –

CAROL:
No, well, it's for Kathie and everyone else, open it –

LIZ tears the wrapping paper off the gift. A small, simply carved wooden figure appears, the figure of a woman or a girl.

FRANK: *(More or less pleasantly interested.)*
Hey – what have we got here?

For LIZ this is a very special moment.

LIZ:
Oh my God. That's so beautiful. Look, a little girl – is that –

She's almost in tears again.

Isn't it beautiful – is this, did Annie choose this? It's so beautiful –

CAROL:

Just stay at home all the time. Never go anywhere.
Never leave the country, not even the city. Get good jobs.
Get pregnant. Have kids. Two or three would be best.

Short pause.

Drive the car out of the garage. Drive the car back into the
garage. That's it.

Short pause.

That would have been it.

1.18.

LIZ:

Isn't it beautiful – is this, did Annie choose this?
It's so beautiful –

She hugs CAROL again.

FRANK:

Cool. Someone's really made that by hand – and that's
what they play with in –

LIZ:

What should we call her?

MARTIN:

Hmh –

LIZ:

Shall we call her Annie?

CAROL:

What, Annie? No, no – we can't call her Annie, Annie is –
Annie.

Short pause. Thinks.

MARTIN:

> Abeni, what about Abeni? That sounds a bit like Annie but it's different –

> Abeni.

LIZ:

> Abeni? Does that mean something?

MARTIN:

> Abeni. I don't know, it sounds nice, I always liked –

FRANK:

> Or Abeni-Annie. Or Annie-Abeni.

MARTIN:

> Ok – that's alright, Carol, isn't it? Annie-Abeni.

LIZ: *(Celebratory.)*

> Annie-Abeni...I don't know, or is just Abeni better? Welcome.

> *LIZ puts the figure on a low table. Next to it lies the Peggy Pickit doll which CAROL already mentioned.*

LIZ:

> Now you can see everything and hear everything.

> *She puts on a voice to act out the Peggy Pickit doll greeting the wooden doll.*

PEGGY PICKIT:

> 'Hello, hello, Abeni,
> I'm Peggy, Peggy Pickit, it's nice to see you.'

> *Short pause.*

> 'So what did you do today?'

ABENI:

> 'Oh, nothing special really. First I was wrapped up in old paper and then put in a bag and then the bag was put in a car and then in a plane and then in another plane and then another plane and then I was here. Hello.'

Short pause.

LIZ: *(With her own voice again.)*
> I've missed you so much. You've no idea how much
> I've missed you. You really were so far away.

1.19.

CAROL:
> The way they had everything lined up: the job, the car,
> the house, the child –

Short pause.

> Like it's all so natural.

Short pause.

> And she really went for him. She just wouldn't stop
> shouting at him.

Short pause.

> She'd baked some bread, fresh bread, to celebrate our
> homecoming. It smelt delicious.

1.20.1.

LIZ:
> I've missed you so much. You've no idea how much
> I've missed you. You really were so far away.

CAROL: *(Not meaning this criticism seriously.)*
> Hey – You were going to come and visit us, you said at
> the airport you'd come and visit us, just before we went
> through security, just before you started crying.

LIZ: *(Laughs.)*
> Yeah – yeah, it's true, isn't it, Frank, we did say that,
> and we did want to –

FRANK:

I always wanted to – well, for me it would have been –
I always thought that I'd or we'd, if we didn't –

LIZ:

But then I got pregnant – and with the baby –

FRANK: *(Shrugs his shoulders.)*
The baby – that is the downside of having kids –

LIZ:

It's not so easy traveling with a baby – simply because of
the vaccinations –, you know all the things you've got to be
vaccinated against – the whole list –

CAROL: *(Waves this away.)*
Yeees, but – the thing about vaccinations –

LIZ:

Yellow fever, malaria, typhoid. Hepatitis A.
Hepatitis B. You've got to have them all –

CAROL: *(Tries to put the danger of infection in perspective.)*
Yeees, but –

MARTIN:

Of course – you've got to have vaccinations or you would
have had to, especially small children – we did them
ourselves, if we had the vaccines and if – assuming we did
have them – they hadn't gone off, because we couldn't
always keep them cold enough –

CAROL:

Yes but it depends on where you're going to be and what
you're – I still haven't had a hepatitis B jab to this day –
have I?

1.20.2.

FRANK:

They'd both refused to let themselves be examined.

Short pause.

They'd both refused to have blood tests.

1.20.3.

CAROL:

Yes but it depends on where you're going to be and what you're – I still haven't had a hep B jab – have I?
(*To* MARTIN.)
Have you had a hep B jab? Have we been vaccinated against hepatitis?

MARTIN:

No, they're right, they are right, you've got to have vaccinations. And the last time I had a typhoid jab it practically killed me, at least that's what it felt like –

FRANK:

Mmmh, I know, it has that effect on a lot of people, but – hey – it's a lot better than typhoid –

Short pause. Joking.

Did they put you in quarantine, you ought to have four weeks in quarantine.
Who knows what you're bringing in with you. What you're dragging in here.

Laughs at his own fantasy.

1.21.

LIZ:

Neither of them looked good, they were tanned, yes, but tired. Or worried. They'd both lost weight. Especially him: It was almost as if he had some sort of disease.

FRANK:

You ought to have four weeks in quarantine.

Who knows what you're bringing in with you. What you're dragging in here.

Laughs at his own fantasy.

MARTIN:

Ridiculous – the jab almost killed me and then there wasn't a single case of typhoid the whole time.

CAROL:

Like I was just saying: it's all completely – everyone's absolutely obsessed – like it's all terrible, like there's nothing but – there wasn't a single case of typhoid the whole time –

FRANK:

What about this: maybe Abeni here's carrying all kinds of infections, straight into quarantine –

LIZ plays with the dolls.

PEGGY PICKIT:

'Hello, hello, Abeni, are you sick? It's off to quarantine with you!'

Brief moment of silence.

FRANK: *(Seriously.)*

So how're you doing, now that you're back –

1.23.

MARTIN:

They'd both got fatter, put on weight. They weren't fat, hadn't lost their shape, they were just: plump. And pale.

Brief moment of silence.

FRANK:

So how're you doing, now that you're back –

Pause.

What was it like?

MARTIN: *(Laughs.)*
Horrific.

CAROL: *(Almost at the same time.)* Wonderful.

She boxes him playfully.

Stop it! Stop it!

MARTIN: *(Laughs.)*
It was horrific, horrific, which doesn't –

CAROL takes MARTIN's hand.

CAROL:

It was wonderful.

2.1.2.

MARTIN:

Everyone laughs.
And I have another drink.

2.1.3.

CAROL:

It was wonderful.

Everyone laughs at these contradictory views.

MARTIN:

(Hand in hand with CAROL.) No, actually it was really nice.

MARTIN has another drink.

CAROL:

Or horrific? I don't know.

She smiles. She lets go of his hand.

2.2.1.

FRANK:

He was drinking faster than everyone else but that was
nothing unusual, he always had done.

2.2.2.

LIZ:

He'd cheated on her, with one of the nurses, this eventually
came out that evening, when she was crying in the kitchen,
we had a brief moment to ourselves in the kitchen, just the
two of us, and she'd cheated on him too, he said later, with
a doctor from Montreal, Rob or

French pronounciation.

Robert, who'd also been involved with the nurse at some
point. Before. With the nurse Martin was involved with.
Later.

Short pause.

Their relationship had almost completely broken down.

Short pause.

FRANK:

A total disaster.

2.3.

MARTIN: *(Hand in hand with CAROL.)*
No, actually it was really nice.

MARTIN has another drink.

CAROL:

    Or horrific? I don't know.

    We weren't welcome everywhere –

FRANK:

    Weren't you?

MARTIN:

    Well –

CAROL: *(Smiles at LIZ.)*

    I think it was wonderful and horrific. At the same time.

    It's just difficult. They're difficult circumstances.

    Smiles at LIZ.

    It wouldn't have suited you –

LIZ: *(Protesting.)*

    Why – why wouldn't it –

CAROL: *(Knowing.)*

    Oh, well –

LIZ:

    Why –

CAROL:

    Because of the spiders.

LIZ:

    Ugh. Spiders.

    Short pause.

    Big spiders?

CAROL:

    I'm saying – it wouldn't necessarily have been a place for

    you, would it, Martin?

MARTIN:

    Big.

    Short pause.

Really big.

CAROL: *(Laughs.)*
Huge spiders.

LIZ: *(Shivers imagining them.)*
Uuughh.

CAROL uses her hand to imitate a spider which approaches LIZ and crawls up over her. LIZ screeches and loses control for a short time.

LIZ: *(Shouts.)*
Stop it! Stop it! Stop it!

2.4.

MARTIN:
An absolute nightmare.

Short pause.

Carol slapped Liz in the face with the flat of her hand, as hard as she could.

CAROL slaps LIZ in the face.

2.5.

LIZ screeches and loses control for a short time.

LIZ: *(Shouts.)*
Stop it! Stop it! Stop it!

Suddenly rather drunk, over the top, with a mixture of fascination and revulsion.

Uuughh, – it's like in that film when this guy stabs himself in the ear with a pair of compasses because some animal's crawled inside there, a spider or a beetle or something and he can't get it out but he can hear this spider crawling round inside his head all the time, I'll never forget the way he stabs the compasses right into his ear, and what he really wanted to find was the source of the Nile or something like that.

That's the only reason, the only reason why I couldn't go, because of the spiders, and because of the –

MARTIN: *(Drinking happily.)*
The spiders, the snakes, the mosquitoes.

And another delightful topic of conversation is the way healing processes are affected, it really is like they tell you, you'll get a little cut somewhere and the wound just won't heal up, it drives you mad –

FRANK:
Hm.

MARTIN:
It just won't heal.

Short pause.

CAROL:
Cockroaches. Cockroaches –

LIZ: *(Disgusted.)*
Cockroaches?

MARTIN:
I've seen cockroaches before, like in Brazil, but these ones –

Short pause.

They were really like this big:

He demonstrates a span of around ten centimetres.

This big. And this fat.

He demonstrates a span of around three centimetres.

LIZ:
Aaaaah.

2.6.

FRANK:
What she called the 'letter' was still in her hand.

He screws up his mouth.

And the two dolls were on the table, the wooden Annie-Abeni and Peggy Pickit.

2.7.

MARTIN: *(Demonstrates a span of around ten centimetres.)*
This big. And this fat.

He demonstrates a span of around three centimetres.

LIZ:
Aaaaah.

She examines the doll on the table.

Is this wood, of course, someone's carved it, and look at this: a blue hairband, she's got a blue hairband.
Haven't you got a lovely hairband, Annie-
Abeni, where did you get that, it's really beautiful –

CAROL:
What's that you've got there?

LIZ:
What?

CAROL:
The piece of paper you've got there, what is it, is it a picture?

LIZ:
This –

Laughs partly embarrassed, partly proud.

It's a letter.

MARTIN:
A letter? Who from?

LIZ: *(Laughs secretively.)*
From Kathie –

MARTIN:

From Kathie to you? That's nice –

LIZ:

No, the letter's not to us, the letter is to Annie –

2.8.

CAROL:

She was still holding this letter in her hand and he and he, he screwed his mouth up, just for a moment. He seemed to find it embarrassing. His daughter's letter. He seemed to find the whole thing embarrassing. His wife was embarrassing. His child was embarrassing. The letter was embarrassing.

Short pause.

And it was embarrassing.

Short pause.

Unbearable.

2.9.

LIZ:

No, the letter's not to us, the letter is to Annie –

MARTIN:

To Annie?! That's nice – are you going to show it to us then –

FRANK:

No, I mean, apart from the spiders and the mosquitoes – honestly – what was it like? What was it really like?

2.10.

LIZ:

And then it turned out that Martin had cheated on Carol with a local girl, a nurse, and that she'd also cheated on him with one of their colleagues, a doctor from Montreal, Rob or

French pronunciation.

Robert.

2.10.2.

CAROL:

And then the stupid girl turns round and says she's pregnant.

2.10.3.

MARTIN:

She slapped her.

FRANK:

She slaps her.

CAROL slaps LIZ in the face. Pause.

MARTIN:

And Liz hit her back.

FRANK:

And then, after a second's shock, Liz hit her back.

LIZ hits back.

CAROL:

I never thought she'd hit me back.

FRANK:

The evening was a total disaster.

2.11.

LIZ:

No, the letter's not to us, the letter is to Annie –

MARTIN:

To Annie?! That's nice – are you going to show it to us
then –

FRANK:

No, I mean, apart from the spiders and the mosquitoes –
honestly – what was it like? What was it really like?

CAROL: *(Thinks about this.)*

Different. Different from what I expected.

It really wasn't easy.

She counts.

There's no electricity.

When it rains: no roads. What do you do when there's no
road? No roads, no cars.

No cars – no transport. Basically: no economy. And apart
from that: no communications. No telephone.

Short pause.

That there are places that cannot be reached by any means
– that that's still possible – I didn't realize –

FRANK:

Great.

Short pause.

MARTIN: *(Laughs.)*

Yeah – apart from that it was pretty much like everywhere
else: yellow fever, malaria, hepatitis A, hepatitis B, the
whole fucking menu. Every kind of shit you can think of.

And of course –

He makes a helpless gesture with his hands –

The disease of all the evil spirits.

Short pause.

There are a lot of people dying.

FRANK:

Well, yeah, sure. I mean, that's what you were there for –
that was the reason for going.

Short pause.

CAROL:

That's why you didn't want to come, admit it –

LIZ:

No –

FRANK:

Yes it was – with the baby, yes, yes, of course –

LIZ:

No –

FRANK:

Yes, of course it was, how could we do that to a child – and
what would it have gained from that, what would we have
gained from that, it's true, it's a shame, but that's the way
it is –

CAROL: *(Rather too loud, rather too forceful.)*

What do you think, d'you think there aren't any children
living there –

2.12.1.

MARTIN:

Rather too loud, rather too forceful. Maybe it was a bit too
loud.

2.12.2.

LIZ:

I'd baked fresh bread and cooked some vegetables,
nothing fancy, I didn't want to spend all my time in the
kitchen.

Short pause.

At first I thought I'd do something African, ok, it's obvious
– I honestly didn't know what –
The main thing was I didn't want to spend the whole time
in the kitchen while everyone else was having a good time,
so I'd thrown something in a pan in the afternoon.
Something that would be just as good cold.
Celery, olives, capers, raisins.

Short pause.

A parmesan and mushroom salad. And fresh home baked
bread – as a gesture to celebrate their homecoming.
All very simple.

2.13.

CAROL: *(Rather too loud, rather too forceful.)*
What do you think, d'you think there aren't any children
living there –

FRANK:
No, no, of course not, sorry, of course not –

Short pause.

CAROL:
Sorry – sorry –

FRANK:
No, no, you're right –

CAROL:
Still, I'm a bit –

LIZ:
No problem, no problem.

FRANK:
Wine? More wine anyone?

MARTIN:
Please –

Short pause.

Great.

Short pause.

And Kathie's going to school now.

FRANK:

Yes, when this summer's over she's going to start school.

Short pause.

But she can do everything already, she's a bright kid, a real live wire, she can add up and she can write.

MARTIN: *(Joking and happy with glass in hand.)*

What? She can write already? Where did she learn that? It's not like you're so fantastically intelligent –

To FRANK.

You still don't know how to read and write properly.

CAROL: *(Joking amicably, possibly boxing with him again.)*

Idiot. You idiot! What is this in aid of, that's enough now, you want me to start now –

LIZ:

She's written Annie this letter, I've got to read it to you, here, she wrote it herself – she's five, five, I mean

Laughing.

sometimes she scares me.

FRANK:

I have no idea, she's definitely not got it from me, you're right about that, I was a complete failure at school, but she – I don't know, she can read and write, just like that –

CAROL:

Just like that –

LIZ:

This is the letter and she wants to send her doll, her
favourite doll, Peggy Pickit, you won't have seen her,
she didn't exist when you left, I think, look at this –
unbelievable – it's all rubber – look at this thing –

Putting on voices she plays with the two dolls.

PEGGY PICKIT:

'Hello, hello Annie-Abeni, I've written you a letter.'

ANNIE-ABENI:

'You've written me a letter – what for, you think I'm
interested in your letter, what am I meant to do with this
letter?'

PEGGY PICKIT:

'Well, read it, you stupid cow'

ANNIE-ABENI:

'But I don't understand your language anyway.'

PEGGY PICKIT:

'Then someone will have to TRA-NS-LA-TE it, you
moron.'

2.14.

MARTIN:

She'd been holding that letter in her hand the whole time.

Short pause.

And he was embarrassed by it.

Short pause.

Frank with a child – I don't think he was the one who
wanted a child. She wanted the child. And presumably she
was the one who looked after it. I don't think he had any
interest in that child at all.

LIZ:

I thought that they would adopt the girl. Annie. And bring her back with them. I was absolutely sure they'd bring her with them.

Short pause.

Later she shouted at me:

You can't just take a child, how can you – you can't simply say this is my child now, how are you going to get her over the border, without a passport, without a name –

CAROL: *(Suddenly shouts.)*

You can't just take a child, how can you – you can't simply say this is my child now, how are you going to get her over the border, without a passport, without a name –

LIZ putting on voices.

PEGGY PICKIT:

'Hello, hello Annie-Abeni, I've written you a letter.'

ANNIE-ABENI:

'You've written me a letter – what for, you think I'm interested in your letter, what am I meant to do with this letter?'

PEGGY PICKIT:

'Well, read it, you stupid cow'

ANNIE-ABENI:

'But I don't understand your language anyway.'

PEGGY PICKIT:

'Then someone will have to TRA-NS-LA-TE it, you moron.'

Short pause.

MARTIN:

Annie always really loved getting the things you sent in the post – really, thanks for everything –

LIZ:

No, no, thank you, thanks for being able to help.

FRANK:

Of course we'll carry on sending...

LIZ: *(Is amused by her husband's sudden political activism.)*
'We' 's a good one –

FRANK: *(Irritated.)*
You, ok, you –

LIZ:

I'm not criticizing – I know you've got other –

FRANK:

You're the one who sends things, I don't, but –

LIZ:

Yes, of course, all you need to do is tell us who we should send things to now, who to address them to, to make sure she really does get them –

FRANK: *(In a good mood.)*
How is she anyway? How's school?

3.3.

CAROL:

I couldn't tell them – I just couldn't.

Short pause.

I would have taken her, there's nothing I would have loved more – nothing –

MARTIN:

She's holding that letter in her hand the whole time talking

about her daughter, daughter, daughter, her daughter,
this prodigiously gifted child –

3.4.

FRANK: *(In a good mood.)*
How is she anyway? How's school?

LIZ plays with the two dolls.

PEGGY PICKIT:
'Hey? Hey, how are you?'

ANNIE-ABENI:
'I'm good, good, thank you, how are you?'

PEGGY PICKIT:
'Oh, I'm great, I'm sleeping over at my friend Britt's
house tonight and my Daddy says Britt is made of plastic,
hahaha, and he doesn't seem too sure about me either,
whether I might not be made of plastic too, but, I think
we're made of blood and bones. How about you?'

ANNIE-ABENI:
'Me? I'm made of wood, someone carved me.'

PEGGY PICKIT:
'No, no no no, you've got a blue hairband, you're not
made of wood, you're made out of blood and bones!'

3.5.

FRANK:
Tears. Tears of anger. I should have seen them. Or rather:
I did see them – I should have seen them coming.

3.6.

CAROL:
And then she really wants to read the letter, she really does
read the fucking letter out loud.

LIZ: *(As PEGGY PICKIT.)*

'And he doesn't seem too sure about me either, whether I might not be made of plastic too, but, I think we're made of blood and bones. How about you?'

ANNIE-ABENI:

'Me? I'm made of wood, someone carved me.'

PEGGY PICKIT:

'No, no no no, you've got a blue hairband, you're not made of wood, you're made out of blood and bones!'

Short pause. She puts the dolls down.

I mean she wrote the letter herself, all by herself, I mean, isn't it – isn't it charming, and then she packed up all these toys that she wants to send her, and her favourite Peggy Pickit.

CAROL:

Peggy Pickit?

LIZ:

That's what they're called –

CAROL holds the plastic doll in her hand.

LIZ:

And of course I'm saying the whole time that it's silly, because Annie most certainly needs other things than this plastic doll and she might be too old for it by now too, but she's determined to send it – isn't that charming.

CAROL: *(Tries to put the plastic doll on the table but the doll falls over.)* Oh –

LIZ:

It won't stand up by itself, it needs a kind of plastic stand for its feet, look –

MARTIN: *(Interrupts.)* But at the moment we've got no contact with her –

Short pause.

LIZ: *(Laughs incredulous.)*
What?

Short pause.

MARTIN:
We've got no contact with Annie at the moment –

Short pause.

LIZ:
No contact – why not?

Short pause.

No contact. That is disturbing.

MARTIN:
Yeah, it's terrible.

Short pause.

But these things happen, we're just unable to reach anyone, it's no reason to be worried. It happens.

The four of them sit in silence for a moment, thinking.

No, really, it does happen. You've got to understand – it's no reason to be worried, we're used to it, in six years we were cut off a number of times.
It could be the weather. The rain.

He counts, smiling.

No electricity. No roads. And: no communication.
No telephone.

3.8.

CAROL:
Annie wasn't her real name, it wasn't her real name at all, we just called her that –.

She makes an odd movement with her lips.

She didn't say much. She could speak, and she would
say things sometimes, but most of the time she didn't say
anything. And we didn't understand her language – she
could understand us but we couldn't understand her –

No older than seven or eight, I would guess – it's not
easy to guess – She was alone and she wasn't well, so we
looked after her, and ultimately – she didn't seem to have
anybody, she had no money, how could she, no family –
ultimately she stayed with us.

We took her in, not us, the whole team, the whole group,
although head office has a very strict rule against that sort
of thing, they're very firm on that point, but what could we
do, she was sick, she needed medication, daily, at regular
times, or else she wouldn't have lasted six months. Or:
the most she'd have lasted was six months.

Under the medication she improved, but we couldn't
provide for her on a permanent basis, everything had to be
paid for, we couldn't simply give it to her, and we didn't
have enough money, so we wrote to friends, like Frank and
Liz, and they were terrific, really terrific, and they provided
everything: the costs of her care and her food.

The money came, and then the letters arrived.

Hello Annie, how are you?

Hello Annie, we've got a daughter too, Kathie, hopefully
you can get to know her one day.

Hello Annie, just imagine what happened to Kathie today.

LIZ:

Hello Annie, I know that you still need to learn to read and
write but perhaps you'd like to paint us a picture?

That would be awesome.

197

MARTIN:

No communication. No telephone.

Short pause.

LIZ: *(With glass in hand.)*
Still disturbing isn't it?

Short pause. She decides to change the subject.

You look so different, your way of looking has changed so much, you look like people who've seen something –

CAROL:

I don't know, what do people look like who've seen something, what do they look like – ?

Short pause.

We didn't get to see much –
We hardy got out of the compound.
You can't just hop in the car and drive off somewhere, first of all where do you go and second how – it's much too dangerous.

LIZ:

But you have, you've got this faraway look in your eyes.

MARTIN:

We're back here now –

LIZ:

But that look –

CAROL:

Well –

LIZ:

It's sexy. Yeah, sexy.

MARTIN:

Thank you.

LIZ:

You're welcome. Don't mention it.

3.10.

MARTIN:

I always said we couldn't accept the responsibility.

It's not like we had control of the situation. Things can happen at any time. We shouldn't tie ourselves down. That's how dependence develops. On both sides.

3.11.

LIZ:

It's sexy. Yeah, sexy.

MARTIN:

Thank you.

LIZ:

You're welcome. Don't mention it.

CAROL:

But like I said, we didn't get to see much.

Short pause.

We've seen a lot less than you'd think –

Short pause. Laughs at her insight.

The most I actually saw was on the flight home.

FRANK:

After six years –

CAROL:

We couldn't move freely, in the beginning, yes, in the beginning we still did, but it was tricky –

FRANK: *(Laughs.)*

It's like in a –

MARTIN:

We weren't always welcome –

FRANK: *(Laughs astonished.)*
Well –

MARTIN:

We weren't always welcome.

FRANK:

Why not?

Short pause.

MARTIN shrugs his shoulders.

MARTIN:

You can't imagine –

Pause. Another change of subject.

CAROL:

Lovely house.

LIZ:

With a garage. Did you see it? We've got a garage.

Short pause.

Awful, isn't it?

MARTIN:

Why?

LIZ:

A garage is the last straw –

MARTIN:

Why? My parents had a garage.

LIZ:

Exactly, mine too, and now we've got one, it's terrible.

FRANK:

I didn't know what you've got against the garage –

LIZ:

And the car stays in this garage and we keep things, like
winter tyres, for example,

CAROL:

But that's wonderful, I wish we had a garage – I mean, we
haven't even got a house –

Laughs.

A house would do at the moment, wouldn't it?

LIZ:

Or Frank's surfboard is in there, which never gets used
any more, because you can only use a surfboard on waves
which have got surf, but anywhere where there's surf is too
dangerous for Kathie to swim so we can't go on holiday
where there are any waves and the surfboard has spent five
years just hanging on the wall, buried alive: like the garage
is a surfboard mausoleum. Yeah.

And then you spend all day looking at the garage door,
oh, the car's there, Frank's back, or, oh, the car's not there,
Frank isn't back yet, the door is always going up or down,
I mean you're devoting your lives to helping other people
and we're opening and closing the garage door.

3.12.

MARTIN:

It really is like they tell you, you'll get a little cut
somewhere and the wound just won't heal up, it really
drives you mad –

3.13.

LIZ:

And then you spend all day looking at the garage door,
oh, the car's there, Frank's back, or, oh, the car's not there,
Frank isn't back yet, the door is always going up or down,

I mean you're devoting your lives to helping other people and we're opening and closing the garage door.

Short pause.

CAROL:

Sometimes I ask myself whether it wouldn't have been better – if it wouldn't have been better – if it wouldn't have been better if we'd never gone.

Short pause.

LIZ:

What? But why – we all talked about this, they need doctors down there, they need nurses and everyone, everyone stayed here, like us, just like us, except you – that's – that's wonderful –

CAROL:

Yeah, I don't know if you'd think it was so wonderful if you – I mean, we, or I, as far as I'm concerned we're only talking about me here, I'm not speaking for both of us – we've got nothing, nothing at all, no house, no family, at the moment I don't even have a job – ok, all that can change, but I don't have a clue what I'm doing here, and I don't understand what's going on here either, I've lost the plot, I've got to make up the last five six years, and I have no idea how, it's just not possible, I'm not going to manage it – and I don't understand anything any more and to be honest I wonder if it was all worth it, whether it was really worth it –

LIZ:

But of course, you've –

CAROL:

Sure, we helped people, or at least we tried to help but it's not like everyone looks on you with kindness for doing it, or they all say thank you, thank you, it doesn't have to be like that, it really doesn't have to, that's not the point, we helped people and afterwards they go and kill each other and set fire to each other and they would almost have killed us too, and then there's always someone somewhere who thinks they're clever and tells us to fuck off and take our jeeps and our radios with us because we're just full of our own importance and that us being there is only going to make the problems worse, can you imagine!

Short pause.

There are places where the only ones left alive are the children and the old people.

Short pause.

LIZ:

Well –

CAROL:

No, you've really got to try to imagine this –
Like it's our fault – us –

FRANK:

It's obvious –

LIZ:

What's obvious?

FRANK:

Everyone knows it's just a great big job creation scheme.

CAROL:

What?

3.14.2

MARTIN:

The idea wasn't particularly original, it wasn't the first time we'd heard that. It kept cropping up.

3.14.3.

FRANK:

Everyone knows it's just a great big job creation scheme.

CAROL:

What?

CAROL:

What kind of –

MARTIN:

Come on, come on –

3.14.4.

CAROL:

A bit drunk maybe – yeah – but only a little bit –

3.14.5.

MARTIN:

Come on, come on –

FRANK:

You know, of course you know –

LIZ:

What –

CAROL:

No, no –

MARTIN laughs

FRANK:

Whole suburbs full of advisers and volunteers and they get accustomed to the lifestyle –

CAROL:

What kind of lifestyle – what lifestyle –

FRANK:

Oh, come on, the cars –

CAROL:

What cars –

FRANK:

The servants –

CAROL:

What servants? Look, are you – what are you talking
about?

MARTIN drinks.

FRANK:

Splendidly cheerful advisers and volunteers who have the
time of their lives with their servants and they've always
got money in their pockets, money to spend, money that's
power –

CAROL:

Hang on –

FRANK:

And the others –

LIZ:

What are you talking about? You haven't got the faintest idea –

CAROL:

You haven't got the faintest idea!

FRANK:

You can read about this all the time – everyone's been
writing that –

LIZ:

Even if –

FRANK:

If what?

LIZ:

I wouldn't mind you coming out with this kind of stuff if
you'd been there or if you'd been born there –

FRANK:

Why – this neo-colonialism – this is where it comes from –

LIZ:

If you'd been born there –

FRANK:

Something like that.

CAROL:

That's crap, complete and utter crap –

FRANK:

Fine, fine, I've finished –

CAROL:

Complete crap –

FRANK: *(Laughs.)*

I'm not saying anything!

CAROL:

It's crap –

3.15.

FRANK:

And then it turns out that he'd cheated on her, with a girl or one of the nurses –

And she'd cheated on him too, with a doctor from Montreal, Rob or:

French pronunciation.

Robert.

3.16.

CAROL:

It's crap –

Short pause. Everyone calms down.

LIZ:

You really do look different –

CAROL is still thinking about the previous subject and suddenly becomes really angry.

CAROL:

Though – yeah – the time of our lives – yeah, the time of our lives –

3.17.

MARTIN:

It was a mistake going there.

But ok: who knows what would have happened to us if we'd stayed here.

We didn't want children, ever, that was agreed, definitely not. But in other circumstances – who knows.

Short pause.

I was against taking her in.

3.18.

CAROL is still thinking about the previous subject and suddenly becomes really angry.

CAROL:

Though – yeah – the time of our lives – yeah, the time of our lives –

Short pause.

She suddenly screams at MARTIN.

You had to go and fool around with your little girlfriend, didn't you, you just couldn't resist – are you quite sure you didn't catch anything, if I was you I wouldn't be so sure –

Short pause.

And then the stupid girl turns round and says she's pregnant. With his baby.

MARTIN:

Pregnant, how can she be pregnant, how am I supposed to have got her pregnant – She cannot possibly be pregnant by me –

3.19.

FRANK:

And then it turns out that he'd cheated on her, with a girl or a nurse, I didn't quite understand that bit, and that she'd cheated on him too with a doctor from Montreal, and that this doctor, Rob or Robert, had also been involved with this girl or this nurse. Before.

Short pause.

The nurse that Martin later –

Short pause.

And now nobody knows who gave what to whom – or might have done – and nobody is getting tested, nobody is having a blood test. Nobody wants to know.

Short pause.

What a fucking mess.

4.1.

Interlude.

Together the actors tell the audience a story.

MARTIN:

This white back-packer gets to know a girl in Lagos, Adisa,

LIZ:

Adisa?

MARTIN:

Adisa. He thinks Adisa's breathtakingly beautiful, he thinks she's so beautiful, it literally takes his breath away, he's speechless, helpless. He has a feeling that she and he are destined for each other and he tries to get talking to her, he tries to make her laugh, he invites her to dinner, he gives her presents, he does everything he can but she says: 'What's going on, Pumpkin,' she calls him Pumpkin because he's got incredibly bad sunburn, 'tell me what you actually want from me.'

CAROL:

'What's going on, Pumpkin? What do you actually want from me? You look like a pumpkin, did you know that?'

MARTIN:

And he says: 'Adisa, we're destined for each other, you're like a vision, you're the most gorgeous creature I've ever seen.' And she says: 'Stop, Pumpkin, stop.'

LIZ:

'Stop, Pumpkin, stop.'

MARTIN:

And then she says:

Can't you see what's going on?

Why, what is going on, what is it?

Look here, look at my tongue, I'm sick, I'm really sick, and I'm going to die, and so is my mother, and so is my sister, and so is my brother because we've got no money to go to the doctor and there aren't enough doctors anyway and there are no beds and nurses and hospitals and drugs either but most of all more and more people are getting sick because they simply don't know what's going on here and nobody understands that in a couple of years if this carries on there are going to be 20 million less of us. 20 million.

FRANK:

20 million.

MARTIN:

And then the back-packer starts doing something. He buys

a plane ticket, and he flies to New York, and he stands there, in the street, and he talks to people, more and more people all the time, and he tells them what he's seen, he talks about Adisa and how she is, and how her sister is, and her mother and her brother, and that they need help, that something has got to be done, and more and more people listen, at first it's only a few, but then it's a few hundred, then a thousand, then more, and finally, finally he talks to all the heads of state in the world and he tells them: we've got to do something. We've got to help. And now –

Short pause.

Now something wonderful happens. What happens now is so important, so beautiful and is so significant for the whole of humanity – like walking on two legs, for example, or discovering that the earth's not flat or the French revolution or the abolition of slavery –

Something happens that's as wonderful for the whole of humanity as discovering penicillin or developing x-rays or liberating Auschwitz or inventing the light bulb or the telegraph:

Help arrives.

Things start to change, hospitals are built for Adisa and the 20 million others, doctors arrive, medicines arrive, tons of them, at no cost, all paid for by the rich peoples of the earth, and free schools are set up, where the children don't just learn how to read and write, they also learn what they've got to do to stop getting sick, and what happens then?

What happens then is a miracle achieved by all the peoples of the earth acting together:

People stop dying.

The sick suddenly get better. People who thought they'd not live to see another Sunday, get out of bed and start working.

Short pause.

And the man comes back, Pumpkin, who's got incredible sunburn all over again, he's older, but apart from that he looks good, very good in fact, and he meets Adisa, she's still coughing a bit but apart from that she's better than she's been in a long time, and she says: 'Pumpkin, are you going to say you've saved the world just to impress me? I don't believe it: don't tell me, you saved the world just to impress me.'

LIZ laughs, FRANK and CAROL too.

And he says: 'Yeah, sure, what do you think, 'course I did. Adisa. You are the most beautiful person.' And she says: 'That was very kind of you, really, very kind, and I don't want to be ungrateful, but to be honest: it's not going to work out with us, there's someone else.' And he says: 'What? You mean I've got no chance at all? Can we at least walk a few yards hand in hand –'

'No, she says, that's not going to happen.'

He says: 'Have I really not got any chance at all?'

And she says: 'Yes, that's what it looks like, I'm afraid so. Goodbye, thank you and take care.'

Smiles.

5.1.

FRANK:

And it turns out that Carol had cheated on him too, with a doctor from Montreal, and that this doctor, Rob or Robert, had also been involved with this girl or this nurse. Before.

Short pause.

The nurse that Martin later –

And now nobody knows who gave what to whom – or might have done – and nobody is getting tested, nobody is having a blood test. Nobody wants to know.

Short pause.

What a fucking mess.

5.2.

CAROL suddenly screams at MARTIN.

CAROL:

You had to go and fool around with your little girlfriend, didn't you, you just couldn't resist, are you quite sure you didn't catch anything, if I was you I wouldn't be so sure –

Short pause.

And then the stupid girl turns round and says she's pregnant. With his baby.

MARTIN:

Pregnant, how can she be pregnant, how am I supposed to have got her pregnant – She cannot possibly be pregnant by me –

Somewhat irrational.

I mean it's not a question of whether I had sex with her, which I didn't, I did not have sex with her, the question is who hadn't had sex with her, everybody had had sex with her at some point, everybody, except me –
Like Rob, for one.

Imitates her, feigning astonishment.

What, Rob?
Yes, Rob – Your Rob.
From 'Montreal'.
Rob? When?
Before you were with him –

But there was nothing between me and Rob –

Rubbish, I saw it, I saw you,

And before you did it with him – he did it with her, and
who knows, maybe she gave him –

And he gave you –

And you gave me –

It gets around fast, that kind of thing, gets round really fast
– frankly, who knows?

5.3.

CAROL:

I would really have loved to have children. But when I
realized that, it was too late. It's too late now. Or: maybe
it's not too late yet. But it's no longer feasible, it doesn't
make sense any more. It's gone.

5.4.

MARTIN:

It gets around fast, that kind of thing, gets round really fast
– frankly, who knows?

Long pause. FRANK stirs himself and pours more wine.

5.5.

LIZ:

First I thought I'd do something African, ok, it's obvious –
I honestly didn't know what –

The main thing was I didn't want to spend the whole time
in the kitchen while everyone else was having a good time,
so I'd thrown something in a pan in the afternoon.

Something that would be just as good cold.

Celery sticks, olives, capers, raisins.

Pine nuts.

Short pause.

Aubergines, of course. I'd forgotten, you cut them into cubes, put salt on them, leave them to drain for a couple of hours, then rinse them, dry them off and fry them gently. Then you take out the cubes of aubergine, wipe off the pan and braise the other things till the celery is cooked through. Then you put the aubergines back in. Deglaze them with vinegar. Let the vinegar reduce. Then add salt and pepper.

Short pause.

A parmesan and mushroom salad.

Short pause.

Fresh bread. A kind of gesture.

Short pause.

It smelt delicious.

Short pause.

And it's just as good cold.

5.6.

MARTIN:

It gets around fast, that kind of thing, gets round really fast – frankly, who knows?

Long pause. FRANK stirs himself and pours more wine.

FRANK:

Look, I wanted to ask anyway –

Short pause.

Even if at the moment there's – no contact – what we should do about the money, I mean, we should carry on with the transfers, shouldn't we?

Short pause.

I mean, you being back doesn't change anything about –
the situation, we'll carry on sending things, like Kathie's
letter here, and the doll, Peggy Pickit –

LIZ:

You won't know these, they've only been around for a
couple of years, they're really amazing, look, they're these
tiny figures and the things they wear are made of rubber or
latex, incredible, isn't it, all the things you can do this this –

MARTIN:

Well – at the moment – at the moment I wouldn't send
anything –

FRANK:

Why?

MARTIN:

You shouldn't send anything right now, it wouldn't get
there – at least not at the moment –

FRANK:

Why not –

MARTIN:

Because –

LIZ:

But everything's got through up till now, hasn't it? The
things arrived and the letters –

MARTIN:

Yes, but right now – right now, there's no-one there – we
think.

LIZ:

There's no-one there? But there's got to be somebody –

MARTIN:

Temporarily. We think. For the time being.

LIZ:

What?

Short pause.

What about Annie?

MARTIN:

We just couldn't, it got to be –
It was too dangerous.

Short pause.

We just couldn't go on. Nobody came any more, nobody
could get through, the roads weren't safe –

Short pause.

I thought you knew that.

FRANK:

No –

LIZ:

And now?

CAROL:

Now? What about now?

LIZ:

What's happening now –

CAROL:

I don't know. I just don't know. We can't get hold of
anyone.

MARTIN:

It's possible that a couple of the nurses have resumed food
supplies –

CAROL laughs.

CAROL:

It's also possible they haven't. It's possible they've
ransacked everything.

FRANK:

How – but surely you've got to –

LIZ:

But you can't.

CAROL:

I know –

LIZ:

The people have got to have food –

CAROL:

Yes –

LIZ:

If they don't get their medication then the whole treatment
is –

CAROL:

I know –

Short pause.

There was nothing we could do, we had to go –

LIZ:

But – the people –

CAROL:

They were on the verge of –

LIZ:

Oh God.

Silence.

And Annie?

CAROL shrugs her shoulders.

LIZ:

What does that mean? What does that mean?

Short pause.

LIZ:

Why didn't you just take her with you, you couldn't leave her there –

5.7.

MARTIN:

It really is like they tell you, you'll get a little cut somewhere and the wound just won't heal up, it drives you mad –

5.8.

LIZ:

Why didn't you just take her with you, you couldn't leave her there –

MARTIN:

How, how do you imagine that working –

LIZ:

You couldn't just leave her on her own, you just abandoned her to her fate, what's going to happen to her now –

CAROL:

She was away the day that we – perhaps she still had someone, somewhere, a grandmother, an aunt, I don't know, it's still possible that relatives might turn up from somewhere –

LIZ:

Oh right, I thought, she didn't have anybody – who are these relatives you're talking about, there was no-one left, you said so yourself, just the children and the old people, she was left entirely on her own –

CAROL:

You can't just take a child, how can you – you can't simply say this is my child now, how are you going to get that child over the border, without a passport, without a name –

Short pause.

LIZ: *(Reads out the letter.)* 'Dear Annie, I am well. How are you?'

Short pause. She is struggling to keep control.

'I am well. How are you?'

She can't read any more. She throws the letter down on the coffee table.

What do I say to her? What am I supposed to say to her now?

CAROL:

Who?

LIZ:

Kathie.

Short pause.

LIZ:

And what are we going to do with this?

She's still holding the letter in her hand. The two dolls are in front of her.

LIZ:

What are we going to do with that?

CAROL:

I have no idea.

LIZ:

I've got to do something with it. I can't give the doll back to Kathie. Can I?

She becomes more and more agitated.

Should I throw it away? I could just throw it away –

FRANK:

Let's wait a few days –

LIZ:

What's the point of waiting, what is there to wait for,

I don't think she's alive any more – but everyone wants to
pretend.

Pause.

5.8.2

FRANK:

Hey, it's ancient but I got my old record player repaired.
I don't know, I think it must have been broken for fifteen
or twenty years.

It's amazing that the thing works again.

He shakes his head.

I think this record belonged to my parents.

*He puts a record on – presumably something like an old Paul Simon
recording. An alternative could be something from the civil rights
movement like the songs of Pete Seeger ('We Shall Overcome') live
at Carnegie Hall.*

*FRANK, LIZ, MARTIN and CAROL sit in silence, drinking, maybe
smoking and listening to the song.*

Short pause.

5.8.3.

LIZ: *(Increasingly agitated.)*

Everyone wants to pretend.

Short pause.

You don't have to think I'm crazy – just because I'm sitting
here with my child's letter and her doll. There's nothing
to wait for, everyone here knows that, if Annie isn't fed,
fed regularly, that's the point, that was the point, if there's
no-one looking after her, then she's got no chance, not the
slightest, then she's going to die – and we somehow accept
that because it's not apparently within our power to change
that, I mean, even if she is – maybe – still alive, she might

as well be dead already, dead, that's definite, you all know that as well as I do, everyone here knows that as well as I do –

She crumples up the letter, tears the wooden doll and the PEGGY PICKIT *to bits and throws both dolls into the corner.*

Brief hiatus.

CAROL *slaps* LIZ *hard in the face with the flat of her hand.*

LIZ *hits* CAROL *in the face equally hard.*

5.9.

MARTIN:

She'd been so happy. She'd actually cried when we all saw each other. She was really – out of it. She was tremendously excited, she talked too much, and she was so funny, she really was talking rubbish, excited rubbish, just to have something to say, and she knew that, and she said so, actually she was just like she always was – like before.

5.10.

CAROL *slaps* LIZ *hard in the face with the flat of her hand.*

LIZ *hits* CAROL *in the face equally hard.*

5.11.

CAROL:

She said she didn't want to spend the whole time in the kitchen so she'd thrown something into a pan.
Something that we could eat cold.
Aubergines, celery, olives, capers, raisins.

Short pause.

Pine nuts.

Short pause.

A parmesan and mushroom salad. Fresh bread.
She'd baked the bread herself.

Short pause.

It smelt delicious.

5.12.

CAROL slaps LIZ hard in the face with the flat of her hand.

LIZ hits CAROL in the face equally hard.

Nobody says anything. After a while.

CAROL:

Sorry.

Short pause.

I'm really sorry. I apologize.

Short pause.

LIZ:

No, I'm sorry, I apologize.
I want to apologize.

The two women look at each other and hug.

LIZ:

I'm so sorry.

CAROL:

No, I'm sorry, really, I shouldn't have done that, forgive
me.

They hug each other and cry.

FRANK:

D'you want another drink?

MARTIN:

Yeah, go on.

He fills MARTIN'S *glass. He waits for the two women to let go of each other, which they don't do. After a while.*

FRANK:
And what about you two? Another drink?

LIZ: *(Agrees, crying.)*
Mmmhm.

FRANK: *(To* CAROL.*)*
Would you like one too?

CAROL:
Yes, yes please.

LIZ: *(Has almost got to laugh.)*
Terrible, I'm terrible.

She cries again.

Sorry. I'm sorry.

The two women finally let go of each other.

FRANK: *(Trying to be funny.)*
Hey, man. Wow!

He waits for a reaction which doesn't really come.

Wow, like, wow –
Crazy – and all because of –

Short pause.

LIZ: *(Extremely angry.)*
There's no need for you to try to make a joke of everything. There's no need for you to try to lighten the mood.

5.13.

CAROL:
It smelt delicious.

223

LIZ: *(Extremely angry.)*

There's no need for you to try to make a joke of
everything. There's no need for you to try to lighten the
mood.

FRANK:

Hang on a minute –

LIZ:

You don't understand what's going on here,

FRANK:

There's no need for you to shout at me, I've not done
anything to you –

LIZ:

Your presence here is purely physical at best,

FRANK:

What's that supposed to mean – what is this?

LIZ:

You have no idea,

FRANK:

Could you –

LIZ:

You haven't got the tiniest –

FRANK:

Could you stop shouting at me –

LIZ:

You have not got the tiniest idea what is going on here –

FRANK:

Haven't I?

LIZ:

You don't understand, or if you do, then that
understanding doesn't register with you, d'you understand,

do you understand, it does not register with you, you
don't think the thought through, you know, but you're not
at all interested, you are not interested in any of this, all
you want to do is be funny, do you understand, you don't
understand:

*She shouts as loud as she can, she really wants to get this into his
brain.*

The child –

Short pause.

Annie –

Short pause. She shouts as loud as she can again.

The child is – GONE!

Short pause.

SHE'S LOST HER CHILD!

Short pause.

SHE'S GONE!

5.15.

CAROL:

It was actually a really nice idea: fresh, home-baked bread.
So simple. It smelt delicious. The moment we arrived.

Short pause.

She told me how to do it: it's really easy:
500g of flour, 300ml of water, half a cube of yeast, one
or two teaspoonfuls of salt. You make the dough, leave it
to rise for several hours, ideally put in the fridge for eight
hours, then put the whole thing into a pre-heated oven for
20 minutes at 240 degrees.

LIZ:

You don't understand, or if you do, then that
understanding doesn't register with you, d'you understand,
do you understand, it does not register with you, you
don't think the thought through, you know, but you're not
at all interested, you are not interested in any of this, all
you want to do is be funny, do you understand, you don't
understand:

*She shouts as loud as she can, she really wants to get this into his
brain.*

The child –

Short pause.

Annie –

Short pause. She shouts as loud as she can again.

The child is – gone!

Short pause.

SHE–'S GO–NE!

CAROL *stands up and fetches the two discarded dolls,* ABENI *and*
PEGGY PICKIT.

She tries to repair the damaged figures. To do this she roots
around in various drawers in this unfamiliar household and
eventually finds transparent adhesive tape.

*The two women use the adhesive tape to repair the ruined dolls and
the crumpled and torn letter.*

This may take some time.

FRANK:

There's no need for you to shout at me.

Short pause.

I didn't do it.

Short pause.

There's nothing I can do about it – it's not my fault.

Short pause.

There's nothing I can do about what has happened, nobody can – it's not my fault.

The sound of tearing off adhesive tape. Flattening out the paper. The men watch silently and drink.

Finally it's all finished. The Peggy Pickit, the wooden doll and the letter which has been stuck together are all lying on the table once again.

Slow blackout.

The End.

THE FOUR POINTS OF THE COMPASS

The Four Points of the Compass (*Die vier Himmelsrichtungen*) was given its world premiere on 30th July 2011 at the Landestheater Salzburg in a co-production between the Salzburg Festival and the Deutsches Theater Berlin with the following cast:

A Man	Ulrich Matthes
A Young Woman	Kathleen Morgeneyer
A Strong Man	Andreas Döhler
A Woman	Almut Zilcher

Director: Roland Schimmelpfennig

CHORUS

A MAN

A YOUNG WOMAN

A STRONG MAN

A WOMAN

Music.

1

THE YOUNG WOMAN:
>You're Medusa, he says
>and I'm Perseus,
>look at these stars,
>look, curls, like snakes –
>
>Perseus is always linked with snakes,
>because Perseus cut Medusa's head off,
>and Medusa had hair made of snakes.
>Curly snakes.
>
>Hey, says Perseus,
>hey, you've got curls, like snakes,
>you could be Medusa –
>Medusa?
>And I'm Perseus, with the stars,
>who went up to the stars,
>Perseus and Medusa, there's got to be something in that.
>And she goes: you think so?
>Perseus and Medusa? D'you really think so?
>They're just curls.
>
>And she says,
>if you're Perseus
>and I'm Medusa,
>then you'll have to cut my head off,
>hey,
>do you want to cut my head off,
>you can if you want,
>it's always hurting so much anyway,
>
>don't be like that now, not you,
>
>I want to kiss you,
>I want to kiss you,
>he says

THE MAN:

    I want to kiss you,

    I want to kiss you,

    he says

THE YOUNG WOMAN:

    and she says:

    well,

    to be honest:

    I've already got someone,

    but,

    he says, us two,

    we belong together,

    Perseus and Medusa,

    we could

    be a double act,

    no, she says, really –

Short pause.

We walked together along the riverbank,

to the place

where the big wheel is,

and he said,

do you want to go on it,

and I said yes,

and then he asked: Have you been on before?

Yes – does it matter?

No.

Music.

2.

THE WOMAN:

> A woman came from the East,
> she brought snow with her and ice,
> she came by train,
> but the train could go no further,
> because there was so much snow on the track,
> so the woman got out
> and stayed in the city for twenty years.
> I'll see when the next train is,
> she thought,
> as she got off the train,
> She could see into the future,
> just not her own.
>
> *Music.*

3.

THE YOUNG WOMAN:

> Two men,
> hitting each other.
>
> One is shorter, or wirier,
> and the other is stronger and bigger,
> ugly and practically bald.
> Not an equal contest.
>
> The two men hit each other,
> till they bleed,
> and everyone else in the place
> is watching,

the drinkers keep tight hold of their glasses,
and the barmaid
with all the curls
stands to one side with a full tray.

The shorter one started it,
and the other one,
the stronger and uglier one,
doesn't hit back at all to begin with,
he keeps the other one away from his body,

She stretches her arm out with the palm upward.

He keeps the other one away from his body,
with an outstretched arm,
looks like they're dancing,

the bottles are still on the shelf,
the ashtrays are on the tables,
still,
the drinkers keep tight hold of their glasses,

and the barmaid with all the curls
and the full tray stands to one side,

and the short one spits
and kicks
and lashes out –

Short pause.

– spits and kicks and lashes out.

Music.

4.

THE STRONG MAN:
    A man came from the North,

he brought rain with him,

and the forecast
had said:
there won't be a drop today,

the man came by lorry,
and on the platform at the back
he was carrying 400 boxes,
covered with a tarpaulin.

It was raining,
the roads were wet,
and it was already dark,
and the man was driving too fast,
and then
on a bend
the entire load slid off the lorry.
400 boxes
slide off the lorry
and lie there
in a hollow next to the road.
Rain.

Music.

5.

THE MAN:

A man with two tongues.

Short pause.

A man in an oversized, white suit,
white – or white with blue stars,
and with blue hair.

Short pause.

Blue hair.

Short pause.

The man in the rather oversized suit
has blue hair –
It's a wig.

Short pause.

A blue wig.

Short pause.

And his face is white too.
White with make-up, and here,
out of the red left corner of his mouth
there's a little blue tongue poking out,
painted on,
it doesn't look nice,
it really does not look nice.

A blue tongue.
It looks horrible,
especially when the man
opens his pointed mouth,
and his real tongue appears,
the red tongue.
The man seems to have two tongues,
A blue one and a red one.

Good evening,
Says the man with two tongues,
Good evening, and welcome,
I've got some balloons here,

he's got these long tubular balloons,
which you can make into animals, you tie
them, these balloon animals, you know –

238

I've got some balloons here, he says –
that I can turn into anything,
anything you want, a dog, a cat,
or a pig,
or a bird,
or a frog –

Stops momentarily.

or a dog, that's better –
I've got balloons here, he says –
that I can turn into anything, anything,
anything you want –

6.

THE YOUNG WOMAN;

A woman came from the West,
she brought the wind with her,

and today there won't be a breath,
the radio
had prophesied
that same morning,

the woman came over land by coach
and had lots of curls,
the woman got off the bus
and looked for a job
as a barmaid,
and she had mild headaches,
she'd had them for three weeks,
they just wouldn't stop,
nothing could be done,
there was nothing could be done.

7.

THE MAN:

A man came from the South,
He brought fog with him,

and the forecast
had said
it would be a clear night,
a night where you'd have
a good view of the stars,

he came on foot,
he came from one of the estates
on the edge of the city,
early in the morning he was walking
along the road
which the lorries take into the city,
there was fog hanging in the air
and spent fuel,

he found 400 boxes,
400 cartons,
just lying there,
early in the morning,
in a hollow,
by the side of the road, in the fog.

8.

Music.

THE WOMAN:
Early morning:

Madame Oiseau looks in the mirror
and draws round her eyes
with black kohl.

Next to her
her boyfriend,
who she's been
together with for more than ten years.

Madame Oiseau can
predict the future,
she reads cards for money,
she reads palms too
and
– if she doesn't ask the stars –
she can see the future
in a ball of glass.

You will
meet somebody –
or: you will find something.
A great change awaits you,
the cards say you will travel to the
stars,
no need to worry,
life's like that.

And later when on a whim she
lays the cards out,
on a Tuesday morning,
Madame Oiseau,
she says, oh,
oh, she says,
long pause,
someone's going to die today –
today someone will be gone for ever.

9.

THE YOUNG WOMAN:

    The bigger one, the fat one,
    the giant keeps the other one away from his body,
    with an outstretched arm,
    looks like they're dancing,

    the bottles are still on the shelf,
    the ashtrays are on the tables,
    still,
    the drinkers keep tight hold of their glasses,
    and the barmaid with all the curls
    and the full tray stands to one side,
    The men hit each other
    and everyone else in the place
    is watching,

    and the short one spits
    and kicks
    and lashes out –

    Short pause.

9.2.

THE WOMAN:

    Oh, says Madame Oiseau,
    fortune teller,
    someone's going to die today,
    Oh, Madame Oiseau says that morning,
    and looks up from her cards,
    I see a man
    with a bottle,

someone
is going to die today,
someone will be shot.

Takes a sip of coffee,
lays out a couple of cards
and says:
and shortly after seven
you will sell the same man
an animal.

A frog.
He'll buy a frog from you.
A frog. Can you make that?
A frog?

9.3.

THE YOUNG WOMAN:

– spits and kicks and lashes out,

you're still wearing make-up,
says the stronger one, the fat one,
the giant,
come back when you've finished work,
come back when you've got the make-up off,
what do you expect,
I can't fight someone
with make-up on his face,
you're getting blood on your costume,
you'll ruin the stars,
what is it with you,
what's wrong with you,
stop it, stop it.

Music.

10.

THE WOMAN:

Is that the future?
The future is terrible.
But she can't tell her that.

Madame Oiseau
doesn't like her,
she hated her
the moment she came in the door,
Young, curly hair,
let's lay out the cards:
no, let me look at your hand,

the future is terrible.
But she can't tell her that.

Short pause.

I don't know what I should say –
she doesn't like her,
she hated her
the moment she came in the door,
Young, curly hair,

and her husband
will fall
in love with her,
but she doesn't have to look at the cards
lying in front of her
to see that,

I don't know what I should say –

I can only see one thing here:
and now she's already
laying out the cards for the fourth time,

she shuffles, lays them out a fifth time:
she takes the young woman's hand,
and won't let go of it again,
then she says: I can only see one thing here:
curls.
You've got curls.
And the young woman says: curls.
Yes. I know.
Only, the other woman says:
all these curls –
they're also growing inwards.
And won't let go of her hand.

What?
They're also growing inwards,
and your head is full of them.

Music.

11.

CHORUS:

A man came from the West,
37, he brought drought with him,
the fields dried out,
the earth cracked,

and yet there was supposed
to be a good harvest this year,

but the man didn't care,
because he had big plans,
he opened a shop,
that always does business:
an off licence,

he was afraid of nothing,
nothing –
well, practically nothing,
there was just one animal
he was afraid of:

he was afraid of frogs.

He opened the shop,
the off licence,
and got married,
and had a child
and was standing one evening with his wife
and child in front of his shop
in the street watching a man,
who could make animals out of balloons,
what kind of animal do you want,
he said to his son,
and ask him what it costs,
and the boy chose a frog,
for one fifty,

and the father said,
a frog,
are you sure:
wouldn't you rather have a stork,
alright, although he hated frogs –
and then,
it was almost eight, the man said,
I'll just shut up the shop
and then I'll come home,

then a man walked into his shop
who had no face.

12.

THE YOUNG WOMAN:

>The doctor told
>the young woman with curly hair:
>something is growing inside your head.
>Inside your head
>something is getting bigger and bigger,
>and we can't take it out,
>it's already too big.
>
>And now
>she tries to understand
>that time has run out,
>
>she looks at herself in the mirror,
>but you can't see anything,
>anything except curls.
>
>And later,
>when she's behind the bar,
>a man says,
>big, strong, a giant,
>why don't we
>get together,
>afterwards,
>when this place is shut,
>and she says:
>why not,
>yes,
>why not.
>Why not.

13.

THE STRONG MAN:

> I left everything
> as it was,
> the boxes in the mud,
> 400 boxes,
> and I left
> the truck with the
> radio on.
>
> I just left
> the truck there,
> with the radio on
> and the windscreen wipers on,
> and I left the 400 boxes
> in the mud.
>
> I went into town,
> on foot,
> and then
> from the Vietnamese place
> down by the bridge
> I bought a weapon,
> a gun,
> and bullets,
> wrapped up
> in an old shirt,
> forget the 400 boxes
> and forget the lorry,
> and I ordered a large beer
> from a young woman
> with lots of curls,
> I asked her,
> whether we could

get together later,

He pulls out the gun.

And with the gun
I robbed an off licence
and the manager of a slaughterhouse.

He shoots into the air three times.

14.

The man with no face
goes into the first shop
in the street:
it's an off licence.

He says:
this is a gun,
a gun with six bullets,
and a short barrel.
One bullet
from a gun
with a short barrel
at this range
makes a heck of a hole,
the bullet rips everything apart.
Your chest
or your forehead
or your mouth
or your neck –
so give me everything you've got.

Music.

15

THE WOMAN:

It's only her own future
she can't see,
Madame Oiseau,
and she won't ask the stars about it.

For that, she says,
she only has to look in the mirror,
you can see the whole future in the mirror,
and in the mirror she sees
her face, no longer young.

Beside her in the mirror
Of the cramped bathroom,
her boyfriend,
twelve years they've been together now,

Pause.

he's putting on make-up,
he's putting white make-up on his face,
he's done that
since he
found 400 boxes
in a ditch by the road
and then
brought them back to his flat,
and here on the right
the bottom right
he paints himself a blue tongue.

Not long now,
she tells him,
they're both doing their make-up,
he puts white make-up on his face

and she draws a dark line along the top of her eyelids
with kohl,
not long now,
and you'll meet a girl,
or have you already met her,
a blonde, or maybe she's dark,
like me either way – with curls.
But she'll be younger.
Younger than me.

Short pause. Music.

Maybe
you'll fall for her really bad.
You're better off forgetting about it.

And now
she understands
that time has run out,

Forget it right away.
Nothing's going to come of it.

16.

CHORUS:

Friday night,
the bar is packed,
and the barmaid with the curly hair
and the full tray
can't keep up,
the air so thick you could cut it with a knife,
and everybody wants another one,
dim lighting,
and it's loud.

The young woman with the curls
pushes her way through the crowd,
the tray high above her head,
then the door opens,
and some guy comes in,
made-up face, blue hair,
he's selling something,
he's sweating and looks
less than happy,
knackered:
and now
the eyes of
the barmaid
and the man meet.

17.

Music.

THE STRONG MAN:

A man with no face.

Short pause.

The man wears an old suit,
trousers, jacket, waistcoat, black,
a shirt, shoes no longer new,

but the man has no face.
The man has no face
and he's got no ears,
no hair,
he's faceless,
unrecognizable.
No eyes,

no mouth.
Looks terrible,
the man looks terrible –
as if he'd
wiped off his own face.
Wiped it away.

Pause.

It's a stocking.
Over his face
the man is wearing a mask –
he's wearing a see-though stocking
made of nylon.

The man with his face wiped off
has a weapon.
He pulls the weapon
out of the back of his trousers:

He says:
This is a gun,
a gun with six bullets
and a short barrel.
One bullet
from a gun
with a short barrel
at this range
makes a heck of a hole,
Imagine
that bullet hits you in the neck.

18.

THE MAN:

> And then the man starts –
> the man in the white suit
> with two tongues –
> one red tongue, the other blue –
>
> The man with two tongues
> blows up one balloon
> after another,
> and then he ties the balloons,
> one after another, to each other –
> the balloons squeak –
> the man is sweating under his blue hair –

THE YOUNG WOMAN: *(Laughs incredulously. Short pause. Then:)*
> I'd never remember all that. How to do it. With the balloons.

THE MAN:

> And while he's doing it the man with two tongues
> makes a face like this –
> a face,
> like he's gazing into the distance.
>
> And the man turns one balloon
> into lots of tiny balloons,
> which he very gently –
> very tenderly –
> with wide eyes
> which are looking somewhere else entirely –
> allows to sail off on the wind...
> and always those two tongues!
> Like this!

He imitates the expression and posture of the balloon man: he turns his head to the left looking into the distance while with both his hands, which are turned in the opposite direction to the right, he nudges a tiny invisible balloon –

THE MAN:

The balloons squeak,

the man's sweating,

his blue tongue,

his red tongue,

him gazing into the distance.

It takes time.

And then:

It's finished.

Finally the animal is finished.

Short pause.

Finally the animal is finished.

Short pause.

And then,

when nobody wants it – to pay for it –

the man with two tongues says to

the barmaid with all the curls:

Here – for you.

And she says: It's beautiful. Thank you.

THE YOUNG WOMAN:

It's beautiful. Thank you.

19.

CHORUS:

> And the boy chooses a frog,
> for one fifty,
> and the father says,
> a frog,
> are you sure:
> wouldn't you rather have a stork,
> alright, although he hated frogs –
> and then,
> it was almost eight, the man said,
> I'll just shut up the shop
> and then I'll come home,
> then a man walked into his shop
> who had no face.
> The man tells the owner of the
> off licence:
> One bullet
> from a gun
> with a short barrel
> at this range
> makes a heck of a hole,
> the bullet rips everything apart.
> Your chest
> or your forehead
> or your mouth
> or your neck –
> so give me everything you've got.
>
> *Music.*

20.

THE WOMAN:

    Yes, today a man will die

    with a barrel

    or with a bottle,

    says Madame Oiseau,

    and before that he'll buy a frog from you,

21.

CHORUS:

    And the other one,

    37, from the West,

    the off licence owner,

    who brought six weeks of drought with him

    and who feared almost nothing in the world,

    tells the fat man,

    the strong one,

    the giant:

    You know what you look like,

    with that stocking over your head,

    you look

    like an animal,

    you look

    like an animal

    without any ears,

    you look like a frog,

    you look like a frog with no face,

    and now

    he understands,

that time has run out,

I hate frogs,
says the shop owner,
they're ugly,
and they're cowards,
and their tongues fill up
their entire bodies
their bodies are full
of their tongues,
and they've got no faces,
they don't know where they should be living,
they're constantly changing their form,
my favourite animal is the stork,
and then the alarm goes off.

22.

THE WOMAN:
Down by the bridge
stands a man from Vietnam,
waiting,
always,
and then a big man comes,
the fat one, the giant,
it's raining,
the man brings the rain with him,
and the man from Vietnam,
names a price and receives
a bundle of notes,
and then he gives
the giant a weapon,
a gun with bullets,

all wrapped up
in an old shirt.
Wait, the Vietnamese man says,
here, and he gives the man
something else, a stocking
made of nylon.

23.

THE YOUNG WOMAN:
The fat man is the fat one –
the strong man, the giant,
comes in,
has a drink,
and one night he says:
come on, let's do something together,
and then they both,
the fat man and the woman with the curly hair,
go down to the river and he buys
two tickets
for the big wheel,
and when they reach the top,
she says to him,
it's nice up here,
just a shame the thing's turning,
it takes you up,
but then it brings you back down again.
And the fat man wonders
whether he should
kiss the girl now,
and she says,
come on,

kiss me,
that's why you brought me up here,
time's running out,
and it would be a shame
if we didn't do it now,
now,
while we're still up here.

24.

THE FAT MAN:

He shouts and spits and lashes out,
and shouts:
don't touch her, don't touch her –
and I go:
why not, she likes it,
you see, she likes it,
she enjoys it,
she's not like you think,
and she's standing there, to one side,
with a tray full of glasses.

Short pause.

She's not like you think,
sometimes she really
wants to be touched, yeah?,
and the fat man,
the strong one, the giant,
winks at the barmaid with all the curls,
and the short man
with the blue tongue
and the costume

covered in stars
loses it.

Short pause. Music.

The short man
with the blue tongue
and the costume
covered in stars
loses it and kicks and lashes out.

25.

THE MAN:

Hey,
he says,
you don't recognize me,
I was here two days ago –
Two days ago?
she says?
Yes, two days ago –

Short pause.

But you don't recognize me.
No,
did we talk?

No –
but we looked at each other –

In the morning, nobody's there,
the place is empty,
and the TVs are on
with the sound off,

Looked – you know

I get people drinks,
I look at a lot of people,
if I'm going to be honest –

yes, yes, he says,
I didn't drink anything –

She laughs.

Then I definitely didn't look at you.

THE YOUNG WOMAN:
Then I definitely didn't look at you.

THE MAN:
Yes you did –
here, by the door, I'd just come in –

She looks at him.
Don't you remember me –

Were you the one with the make-up –
Yes, that's the one, him,
I knew
you'd remember me,
I looked at you,
and since then
I can't stop thinking about you,
I've fallen in love with you,
what's your name?

Short pause.

Do you think
we might be able to
do something together, you and me?
I don't know –
I, I'm starting a business,
you see,
I'm working at it.
Oh, she laughs,

yes, good idea.
Good idea.

I don't think so.
What?
I don't think we should do something together.
Why not?
Yes –
Yes, what?
You keep looking at me like,
don't look at me like that,
when you look at me like that,
you look as if something's
just about to happen to you,
the blood in your veins
stops,
like you're about to
turn to stone,
you might turn to stone,
look out,
really.
I don't think so –
Yes, really.

26.

THE WOMAN:

Madame Oiseau wakes up one morning,
Thursday morning,
six thirty,
and looks in the mirror,
but there's nothing there.
The mirror is empty.

What's happened?
Shakes her head, rubs her eyes –

Short pause.

There she is. She's back.
She can see herself in the mirror again.
This morning
for a moment
my reflection disappeared.
In the mirror in front of me
the empty room
behind me,
and I –
I wasn't there.

THE WOMAN disappears, vanishes suddenly into thin air.

27.

THE STRONG MAN:
The bullet
hits him in the neck,
just here –
and shatters
his windpipe,
heavy breathing,
and the main arteries,
blood everywhere,
he clutches his neck

He is bleeding.

and now
he understands
that time has run out.

A lot of blood.

28.

CHORUS:

On a rainy day
a lorry takes a bend on a main road
at excessive speed.
Too fast, too fast.
Too fast into the bend.
The lorry stays on the road,
but its load flies off the platform,
400 boxes fly off the platform
of the lorry

Short pause.

and land in a hollow.
400 boxes, stamped:
modelling balloons.
Colours: red, yellow and blue.
Rain.
Slowly it gets dark.

Each box contains 100.

In view: the edge of the city.

The next morning,
still very early,
the fog has lifted:
a man alone, a walker.
A man goes for a walk on the edge of the city.
In a hollow by the main road,
next to an unexpectedly sharp bend,
where severe accidents
repeatedly occur, the man finds
400 boxes, stamped: modelling balloons.
Each box contains 100.

Short pause.

The man starts
carrying the rain-sodden boxes
to his flat.
The trip from the hollow
to his flat
and back again
takes him around an hour and a half.
To begin with he carries
four boxes per trip,
then five,
and then, with more practice,
it's seven.

29.

THE STRONG MAN:

The fat man asks:
is there an animal you especially hate,

THE YOUNG WOMAN:

An animal, the girl with the curls asks,

THE STRONG MAN:

yes, someone told me
he hates frogs,
I love frogs,

THE YOUNG WOMAN:

You fuck like a frog too,

THE STRONG MAN:

well, anyway: which animal can't you stand:

THE YOUNG WOMAN:

> And without thinking very long she says:
> snakes. The snake.

THE STRONG MAN:

> He laughs. Of all things.
> Why?

THE YOUNG WOMAN:

> Because a snake always stays
> the same,
> even when it grows,
> even when it
> grows out of its skin,
> it slips out of its skin,
> how beautiful,
> imagine,
> but then everything
> is as it was before.
> It leaves its old skin behind,
> its skin is new,
> but it's got the same journey ahead of it.
>
> *Music.*

30.

THE YOUNG WOMAN:

> He talked and talked,

THE MAN:

> you're Medusa, he says
> and I'm Perseus,
> look here, the stars,
> look, curls like snakes

Perseus is always linked with snakes,
because Perseus cut Medusa's head off,
and Medusa had hair made of snakes. Curly
snakes.

Hey, says Perseus,
hey, you've got curls like snakes,
you could be Medusa –

THE YOUNG WOMAN:

Medusa?

THE MAN:

And I'm Perseus, the star man,
Perseus and Medusa, there's got to be something in that.
And she goes: you think so?

THE YOUNG WOMAN:

You think so?
Perseus and Medusa? Do you really think so?
They're just curls.

And she says
if you're Perseus
and I'm Medusa,
then you'll have to cut my head off,
hey,
do you want to cut my head off,
you can if you want,
it's always hurting so much anyway,

don't be like that now, not you,

I want to kiss you,
I want to kiss you,
he says

THE MAN:

I want to kiss you,
I want to kiss you,

he says

THE YOUNG WOMAN:

   and she says:
   well,
   to be honest:
   I've already got someone,

THE MAN:

   but, he says, us two,
   we belong together,
   Perseus and Medusa,
   we could
   be a double act,

THE YOUNG WOMAN:

   no, she says, really –

   Short pause.

   We walked together along the riverbank,
   to the place,
   where the big wheel is,
   and he said,
   do you want to go on it,
   and I said yes,
   and then he asked:
   have you been on before,

THE MAN:

   have you been on before?

THE YOUNG WOMAN:

   Yes, does it matter?

THE MAN:

   No.

   Short pause.

   He gets better and better,

269

and it becomes easier and easier for him,
ideas arrive effortlessly,
it's like it's happening by itself,
his hands just do their job,
sometimes he starts
and even he doesn't know
what's going to come out,
a bat, a mouse,
the Eiffel Tower,
a rat,
a magpie,

I can make whatever you want,
a bat, a beetle,
the Eiffel Tower,

all out of air,

look Mum,
look,
that man's got blue hair,
that man's got another tongue
painted on his face,
he looks like
a dog,
he's panting,
look,
how much is that?

31.

THE WOMAN:
   Oh, says Madame Oiseau,
   when she sees the stars in the sky that evening,

tomorrow you'll sell something,
a stork and a cat,
tomorrow evening,
twenty past seven
on the corner of such and such
and such and such
a man who's a bit too fat
will buy a cat and a stork from you,

and someone is going to die tomorrow,
is that the same man?
I'm not sure,
I can see
a man with a pig.
Or is it a cow? Or a calf?
I can't say exactly –

32.

He kicks and hits and spits,
and the fat one holds him away from his body,
with an outstretched arm,
like this;

He stretches his arm away from his body.

she's not like you think,
sometimes she really wants
to be touched, yeah?

And then the short one,
the weaker one,
hits the other one,
the fatter, stronger one,

almost by accident,
while he's turning around,
turning,
like in a spiral,
the short one hits
the bigger one,
he hits him on the nose –

He spins around in a circle.

The noise.
The noise in his head
When the bone breaks.
Crack.
The pain,
the pain shoots through his head,
the fat man, the stronger one,
the giant can see stars,
and then he loses it,
and he lashes out,
blind with anger,
all he can see is the face
in front of him,
white, with two tongues,
one red,
the other blue,
the little one now hits him
with almost every blow,

and then lots of things get broken,
the tray of beer,
tables are knocked over, glasses,
bottles,
a mirror goes flying.
There's shouting.

33.

THE MAN:

    The man opened one of the boxes,
red.
Red rubber.
Instructions for beginners:
the god, the cat, the swan.
It's like they make themselves.

He carries box after box
to his flat
400 of them with 100 each,
that takes time,
and the instructions
are in every box,
and in one box
he finds a costume decorated with stars,
a special gift
to make your party a success.

The dog, the cat, the spider.
Out of thin air.
If I sell a dog for
let's say –

twenty of them or,
thirty a day,
for twenty days,
that makes –

and all out of thin air.
Out of thin air.

34.

THE STRONG MAN:

    And then one night the strong man,
    the fat one,
    the giant
    dreamt of his death,
    he dreamt
    of complete darkness,
    there, inside his dream,
    even with his eyes wide open
    he could see nothing at all,
    nothing,

    that
    someone said,
    is the human pyramid,
    look,
    the human pyramid,

    and then he was afraid,
    and he got so afraid,
    that his heart
    almost stopped,
    if I didn't have the gun,
    and then he turns round
    and puts his tongue
    into the ear
    of the woman with curly hair sleeping next to him,

    but she didn't wake up,
    instead she dreamed,
    something
    had crept into
    her head,

and then she woke up
and went into the bathroom
and had a long look at herself in the mirror,
and tried to imagine
what it would be like
what it will be like,
when she's not around any more.
When she's dead.
What happens then.
And she couldn't imagine it,

No matter how hard she tried.
She was afraid.

The human pyramid.

35.

THE WOMAN:
Everyone's selling something.
We're all
trying to sell something.
Either we're selling goods
or skills or strength or time.
But not everyone has something to sell.
And what then?
If someone has nothing to sell,
it becomes hard, because then
he's worth
nothing.
How can anyone live then –
well they have to
if they've got nothing to sell,
neither goods nor skills nor strength,

nothing,
they have to try
to make something out of nothing,
that they can sell.
And if they've got nothing to sell
the only things left
are what they assume
to be free.
Things they find.
Hopes,
lies,
or violence.

36.

CHORUS:

A man came from the North,
he brought a storm with him,
the daylight turned to darkness,
and then
the wind blew the windows in,
who could have predicted that,
he came,
because he'd found
a job here,
that's why he came here,
he travelled
in pursuit of his application,
with a big car
and a lorry full of furniture
and a wife and two children,
a boy and a girl,

both children too fat,
a little too fat,
all four
a little too fat,

and the job
is not just any job,
it is the job of the manager of a slaughterhouse,
a massive job,
every day thousands of dead animals,
have you seen
a chicken bleeding to death,
or a barrow load of raw calves' liver,
I have, oh yes,

and so there they are,
twenty past seven,
standing in front of him,
father, mother, child
and another child

and today the father is
especially generous,
hey big feller,
do you want one of those animals,
what kind of animal do you want,
what kind of animals can you do,
I can make all the animals,
so, what kind of animal do you want –
I – I'd like a cat –
a cat – I hate cats, but never mind,
why, Daddy,
I don't know, always have,
can you do a cat,
and the man
makes a cat –

Short pause.

Now I know
why I hate cats,
why, Daddy,
because cats pretend to be clean,
but they really,
just lick all the dirt off,
they think they're clean,
but all they've done is eat their own
dirt,
and then they throw it up again,
they throw up all their own dirt,
and they all look deceptive, all of them,
but anyway, alright –
and you,
little one, what kind of animal do you want,

me, said the little girl,
I'd like a bird,

a stork, that's my favourite,
yes, Daddy, a stork, storks
are my favourite,
are you sure,
yes, Daddy,
can you do that,
let's see,
you know what I don't like about storks,
no, Daddy,
first they like eating frogs,
and frogs are disgusting,
and second
storks can't make up their minds
where they want to live,
they move here and there,
and they never like it anywhere,

and third
they stick their long beaks
up their arses,
the child cries,
that was a joke, it was a joke,
you know what my favourite animal is,
yes, Daddy,
you know what it is,
yes, Daddy, it's a pig,
a pig, that's right, a pig,
even if nobody else particularly likes them,
no, Daddy,
pigs are much more sensitive
than everyone thinks.
They've got soft skin,
like a person,
they can cry
and like a person
they can die of fear,
imagine that,
storks can't do that,
and neither can cats.

37.

THE YOUNG WOMAN:
And then the short one,
the weaker one,
hits the other man,
the fatter, stronger one,
almost by accident,
while he's turning around,

turning,
like in a spiral,
the short one hits
the bigger one,
he hits him on the nose –

He spins around in a circle.

The noise.
The noise in his head
When the bone breaks.
Crack.
The pain,
the pain shoots through his head –

Music.

38.

THE WOMAN:

A woman came from the East,
she brought snow with her and ice,
she came by train,
but the train could go no further,
because there was so much snow on the track,
so the woman got out
and stayed in the city for twenty years.
I'll see when the next train is,
as she got off the train,
She could see into the future,
just not her own.

39.

A man came from the North,
he brought a storm with him,
and he became manager of a slaughterhouse,
and he loved pigs,
and at night, when work was over,
he sometimes liked to shut
the giant gate of slaughterhouse himself,
the entrance
that all the lorries would drive through
the next morning,
full of cows and calves and pigs,

there was a man standing in the street,
whose face he couldn't make out,
perhaps he had
no face
or is that a stocking,
is that a gun,
and then the man was afraid,
afraid for his life,
and he started screaming,
loud, in the street,
in front of the gate, under the light,
help, help,
and the man with the stocking,
the fat one, the strong one, the giant,
held his mouth shut
and held the gun to his head,
and now
the man thinks,
time has run out,
and what happens then

and then the man fell
down dead,
with the key to the slaughterhouse
still in his hand,
dead of fright.

40.

THE WOMAN:

    That night
    Madame Oiseau dreams
    of her own future,
    for the first time,
    she dreams
    of her own death.
    In her dream she sees
    a woman and a man,
    and the woman is herself,
    in a very short dress.
    And the man next to her
    is wearing a glittering suit.
    And she's vaguely reminiscent of
    an ice skater –
    only she's wearing high heels –
    Good Evening, says the man in the dream
    next to the woman in the dress,
    I can –
    the man in the suit smiles,
    and the woman in the short dress smiles too –
    she smiles charmingly,
    even though she's really too old
    for a dress like this one,

I can, the man says, with a single movement of my hand I
can –
At this point the man moves his hand –
I can with a single movement of my hand,
with a single movement of my hand,
the man makes the movement with his hand again,
make this woman disappear –

and then he points to Madame Oiseau,
who reminds herself of an ice dancer in her dream and
then:

Spread-out, magical fingers.

There they stand, the man
and the woman with the beautiful legs –

The man, the woman.
The move of the hand:

And the woman in the short dress
has disappeared. The ice dancer's gone!

But
when the man with the smile
makes the movement with his hands
a second time, to make
the woman reminiscent of an ice dancer
reappear –
nothing happens.
Nothing.

Suddenly he's sweating with fear.
Now:

Fingers spread out, magical hands.

He repeats the movement with his hands
one more time, a third time –

Desperate, loud, complaining, looking for help:

Nothing! Nothing happens!
And just
when the man is about to say
that he really
hasn't the faintest idea
how any of this works,
that only she,
the ice dancer, knows how –
There the woman is,
Madame Oiseau,
whose name is really
completely different of course,
and who reminds herself
of an ice dancer in her dream,
she's suddenly back,
there she stands, behind him,
just when he was about to explain himself,
she's back.

And
Madame Oiseau wakes up,
Thursday morning,
six thirty,
her heart is racing with the shock,
she had a terrible dream,
she gets up, goes to the bathroom
and looks in the mirror,
but there's nothing there.
The mirror is empty.
What has happened?
She shakes her head, rubs her eyes –

Short pause.

There she is. She's back.
She can see herself in the mirror again.
This morning

for a moment
my mirror image vanished
In the mirror in front of me
the empty room,
behind me
and I –

I wasn't there.

THE WOMAN vanishes into thin air.

41.

THE YOUNG WOMAN:
She doesn't love him,
but she does it with him,
a lot,
everywhere, in the kitchen at the back,
and on top of the bar,
when nobody else is there,
and in the yard
next to the bins,
on her break,
and once even
on the big wheel,
that was funny,
and they had to be quick,
standing.

42.

THE MAN:

I was standing by the kerb,
like I always do,
when I'm on a pub crawl,
I'm standing by the kerb,
it was still midday,
there was a fairground
somewhere, no-one buying anything:
then I saw a pretty big bird,
a magpie,
that was in the middle of the road,
fighting a rat.
A lot of people stood still and watched.
The rat
could hardly move,
but it had enough strength left
to catch the bird
anyway
when it attacked with its beak.
And sometimes
the bird would fly up
and sit on a branch
or the roof of a car,
but it wouldn't let the rat out of its sight.
The rat could hardly move.
All just a matter of time.
Why doesn't
the rat run away,
while the bird's sitting on the car,
someone asks.
Rat poison,

someone says, the rat's probably
eaten some poison,
it's not got long left,
maybe a few minutes more.

Short pause.

And what if the bird eats the rat?
Then it'll eat the poison too.

43.

THE YOUNG WOMAN:
> The woman with the curls
> dreams that night
> of her death.
> She dreams
> of a man in a dark suit,
> with thin hair combed back

Short pause.

> the man looks a little like a waiter,
> a little
> like a tired waiter,
> or like a salesman,
> who drives across the country,

Short pause.

> and he's got a sack with him,
> a bloody sack.

> And in his hand
> the man with thin hair holds
> a sword – or a very long saw.
> He's got a saw.

Good evening, says the man,
welcome,
with this saw –
the man points to his long saw –
with this saw –

With this saw I shall now
remove the head of the Medusa.
The man with the saw says,
my name is Perseus,
Perseus is only a stage name of course,
and with this saw,
with this saw,
I have just removed the head
of the Medusa.
Anyone who looks at the head of the Medusa turns to
stone.
I will now
for a brief moment,
the man with the sack in his hand whispers,
I will now
for a short moment
remove the head of the Medusa.

Anyone who fails to close their eyes now,
will be turned to stone forever.

The man reaches into the bag and closes his eyes.

Silence.

Nobody open your eyes, the man says.
If anyone doesn't shut their eyes –
Everyone shuts their eyes.

You can hear a kind of wheezing.
That's right: You can hear a kind of wheezing,
that's Medusa's breathing.

Just don't open your eyes –

Short pause.

And now, the man says,
after maybe
twenty, endless seconds have gone by,
I am going to put the head of the Medusa
back into the sack.

You can now open your eyes again.
It's over.

And she dreams
that the man
puts her head back into the sack
a rough, brown-grey sack,
she can still see the light
falling through the opening of the sack,
but then the man ties the sack shut.

44.

THE MAN:

　　Let's do something,
　　come on, let's do something together,
　　even if it is over, come on,
　　and then the two of them,
　　the man and the woman who can see
　　into the future,
　　go on the big wheel
　　and when they reach the top,
　　she says to him,
　　it's nice up here
　　just a shame the thing's turning,

it takes you up,
but it brings you down again.
And then you get out at the bottom.
And then he wonders
maybe I could
kiss her one more time, a last time,
why not, maybe,
but that moment she's vanished – gone
and he thinks she's jumped,
he thinks she's killed herself.
Here I am, she says,
back again –

45.

THE STRONG MAN:

> The fat man drinks and says:
> you know something,
> I used to deliver
> balloons just like that
> in a lorry,
> just like –

THE MAN:

> These ones –
> The other man asks, the thinner, weaker one

THE STRONG MAN:

> Yes, just like them,
> 100 in a box,
>
> and you know what happened?
> No, says the man with the white face
> and a second tongue,

who looks as if
he can't breathe,

I lost
the whole lot
slid off the lorry –
oh yeah,
yeah, on the edge of the city,
well,
yeah, four hundred boxes,
the entire load
slipped off the platform,
and then?
Then I stopped,
got out,
looked at it,
that pile of boxes by the side of the road,

and then I simply walked away.
That was the most important day of my life.
You know
what the most important day in my life was?
No, I don't know.
How should I know that,
says the fat man,

it was a Friday,
and I was outdoors,
because I couldn't stand
being inside any more,
on the edge of the city, fog,
on foot, still very early in the morning,
practically still night-time,
in a hollow
by the side of a main road
on a sharp bend
I found

a load of boxes,
400 of them,
modelling balloons,

and the fat man says:
no way.
That's what happened.
And then?
Then I took the boxes.

Took them?
On foot, yes.
All the boxes.
Yes.
You took 400 boxes.
Yes. The most important day of my life.

THE STRONG MAN:

The fat man says:
Rain.
The engine and the windscreen wipers and the radio still
running.

Short pause.

In the hollow 400 boxes.
The red brake lights.

You're doing 130
and the sign said 60.

And then:

He makes a gesture.

the load tips off the lorry.

He laughs.

The engine and the windscreen wipers and the radio still
running.

Short pause.

In the hollow 400 boxes.
The red brake lights.
No way, shouts the fat man,
no way,
and now the same balloons
I left there in the mud
come walking through the door.
No way.
I thought
I'd seen the last of them.
What do you want with them!
With them you won't
even get as far as –
if you at least had –
no-one can live like that.

THE MAN:

Why can't anyone live like that,
I live like that, that's how I live,
If I hadn't found the boxes –
I don't know what would have happened to me.
I couldn't have taken it much longer.
The flat. The view from the window.

THE STRONG MAN:

– I wish you'd never found them!
If only you'd never found them!

And then the fat man laughs
and then he says,
show me, show me,
show me what you can do,
there's got to be something
for me in there,
or for you,
he means the woman,

what about
a dog or a cat
or a beetle
or a frog,
and then he grabs the woman
by the curls
and gives her a kiss.

46.

THE WOMAN:
She has
a feeling,
a sense,
that something is going wrong.

She lays the cards
on the table in front of her
and then looks up:
In front of her,
the fat man
who wants to know
what he must do
for a woman to love him,
a woman with a lot of curls.

She says:
I see here
400 boxes and a lorry by the side of the road,
a Vietnamese
down by the bridge,
and an off licence,
and a slaughterhouse.
And a woman with curls.

Stars.

And a man with a blue tongue.

That is your downfall.

She says:

I wouldn't go out today.

Why,

says Madame Oiseau,

didn't you

load the boxes back up again,

why didn't you get back in again,

why didn't you carry on driving.

Why did you

simply leave the lorry by the side of the main road –

47.

THE STRONG MAN AND THE YOUNG WOMAN:

He kicks and hits and spits,

and the fat one holds him away from his body,

with an outstretched arm,

like this:

He stretches his arm away from his body.

she's not like you think,

sometimes she really

wants to be touched, yeah?,

And then the short one,

the weaker one,

hits the other one,

the fatter, stronger one,

almost by accident,

while he's turning around,

turning,
like in a spiral,
the short one hits
the bigger one,
he hits him on the nose –

He spins around in a circle.

The noise.
The noise in his head
When the bone breaks.
Crack.
The pain,
the fat man can see stars,
and then he loses it,
and he lashes out,
blind with anger,
all he can see is the face
in front of him,
white, with two tongues,
the short one now hits him
with almost every blow,
and then lots of things get broken,
the tray of beer,
tables are knocked over, glasses,
bottles,
a mirror goes flying.
There's shouting,
and the fat one
is mostly hitting thin air,
and the gun
falls behind him out of his trousers,
the fat one doesn't even notice,
he hits blindly at the air
full of anger and pain and blood,
the one with the white face

dodges, he's quicker,
hits the fat one again,
and again,
don't touch her, don't touch her,
I told you –

and then he gets too close
to the fat one,
and the fat one hits the short one,
here –

He makes a gesture.

First on the kidneys,
and then here,
between the liver
and the heart,

48.

THE WOMAN:
Madame Oiseau
can see into the future.
She can read the future
from palms,
or she lays down cards
on the table in front of her,

or she sees the future
in a ball
of glass,

only she can't see
her own future,

she says:
it will rain,

all day long.

And she says:
Oh.
Oh, Oh,
someone's going to die today,
today
someone will be gone for ever.

49.

THE MAN / CHORUS:

He kicks and hits and spits,
and the fat one holds him away from his body,
with an outstretched arm,
like this:

He stretches his arm away from his body.

she's not like you think,
sometimes she really
wants to be touched, yeah?,

And then the short one,
the weaker one,
hits the other one,
the fatter, stronger one,
almost by accident,
while he's turning around,
turning,
like in a spiral,
the short one hits
the bigger one,
he hits him on the nose –

He spins around in a circle.

The noise.
The noise in his head

When the bone breaks.
Crack.
The pain,
the fat man can see stars,
and then he loses it,
and he lashes out,
blind with anger,
all he can see is the face
in front of him,
white, with two tongues,
the short one now hits him
with almost every blow,
and then lots of things get broken,
the tray of beer,
tables are knocked over, glasses,
bottles,
a mirror goes flying.
There's shouting,
and the fat one
is mostly hitting thin air,
and the gun
falls out of his trousers behind him,
the fat one doesn't even notice,
he hits blindly at the air
full of anger and pain and blood,
the one with the white face
dodges, he's quicker,
hits the fat one again,
and again,
don't touch her, don't touch her,
I told you –

and then he gets too close

to the fat one,
and the fat one hits the short one,
here –

He makes a gesture.

First on the kidneys,
and then here,
between the liver
and the heart,

and the short one,
the weaker one,
the man with two tongues
hears a noise inside his body,
something breaks inside his body,
he can't get any air,
and he falls backwards,
onto his back,
tries to hold on as he's falling,
pulls a table over with him,

broken glass, beer on the floor,
blood,

and in the middle
the shorter man,
he's lying on his back,
and he's warm and cold
both at the same time,

his eyes search
for the girl with the curls,

what's the matter with you,
what are you doing,

and then
he stops breathing.

Faces

bend over him,
people
he doesn't know
and the young woman with the curls,
you and me, he thinks,
and the fat one, the stronger one,
the giant
who had kissed her,
whose
nose he'd broken,
I'd like to
break your nose again,

he keeps saying,
you broke my nose,
you broke my nose,
and

what are you doing,
what are you doing,

and
now he understands
that time's run out,

that there is no more,
he forces his eyes open,

there are
the woman with the curls,
the fat man, the stronger one, the giant,
and his wife,
Madame Oiseau,
Oh,
she says,
oh,

he can't breathe,
and he can't

see properly any more,
can't go on,
the faces have gone,
come back,
they're gone again,

Madame Oiseau,
the giant,
and the woman
with the curls

don't touch her, don't touch her,

in the hollow 400 boxes.

You're doing 130 and
the sign said 60.

And then:
The load tips off the lorry.

His eyes
stay open,

he tries to breathe
and can't,

what happens now,
he thinks,

no air,
no air,

his heart
is racing
and almost stops,
his eyes stay open,

And sometimes
a bird flies high
and lands on a branch
or on the roof of a car.

All just a matter of time.

Why doesn't
The rat run away
While the bird's sitting on the car.

It's nice up here,
just a shame that the thing's turning,
it takes you up,
but then it brings you back down again.

And then
it doesn't go any further –

and now
he understands
that time has run out.

Music.

50.

THE STRONG MAN:

A man came from the North,
he brought rain with him,

and the forecast
had said:
there won't be a drop today,

he shot
the owner of an off licence,
and he attacked the manager of a
slaughterhouse,
who died of shock.

The man was tall, strong,
or fat, a giant,

he fell in love with a woman
with a lot of curls,
but who didn't love him
only slept with him
or fucked as she called it

and one day a man with a made-up tongue
broke his nose in a fight,
and then the strong man,
the fat one, the giant
hit the man with the two tongues
here and here and here
and the man with two tongues
died
on the floor of a bar,
and the fat man
stood there,
as if turned to stone,
and couldn't get away.

51.

THE YOUNG WOMAN:
A woman came from the West,
she brought the wind with her,

and today there won't be a breath,
the radio
had prophesied
that same morning,

the woman came over land by coach
and had lots of curls,
the woman got off the bus
and looked for a job

as a barmaid,
and then two men
fell in love with her.

One of them died.
She had headaches,
always,
they just wouldn't stop,
nothing could be done,
there was nothing could be done,
and then she went to the hospital
and nobody ever saw her again.

52.

THE WOMAN:
A woman came from the East,
she brought snow with her and ice,
she came by train,
but the train could go no further,
because there was so much snow on the track,
so the woman got out.
I'll see when the next train is,
she thought.
She could see into the future,
just not her own.
And twenty years later
she stood on the same platform,
the train drove in,
and when the train left again,
the platform was empty.

The End.

WWW.OBERONBOOKS.COM

Follow us on www.twitter.com/@oberonbooks
& www.facebook.com/oberonbook